Getting Our Bodies Back

Getting Our Bodies Back

Recovery, Healing, and
Transformation through
Body-Centered Psychotherapy

Christine Caldwell

Foreword by Gay and Kathlyn Hendricks

Shambahala   Boston & London   1996

Shambhala Publications, Inc.
Horticultural Hall
300 Massachusetts Avenue
Boston, Massachusetts 02115
www.shambhala.com

9 8 7 6 5 4 3

Printed in the United States of America

♾ This edition is printed on acid-free paper that meets
the American National Standards Institute Z39.48 Standard.

Distributed in the United States by Random House, Inc.,
and in Canada by Random House of Canada Ltd

Library of Congress Cataloging-in-Publication Data

Caldwell, Christine, 1952–
    Getting our bodies back: recovery, healing, and transformation
through body-centered psychotherapy / Christine Caldwell; foreword
by Gay and Kathlyn Hendricks.
        p. cm.
    Includes bibliographical references
    ISBN 1-57062-149-7 (alk. paper)
    1. Compulsive behavior—Treatment. 2. Substance abuse—Treatment.
3. Mind and body therapies. I. Hendricks, Kathlyn. II. Title.
RC533.C34 1996   95-41225
616.86'0651—dc20   CIP

To my parents,
Jim and Lucille Caldwell

To my teachers

Allegra Fuller Snyder
Judith Aston
Thich Nhat Hanh

To my friends

Sophie Darbonne
Gay and Katie Hendricks
David Silver
Jayne Satter
Jack Haggerty

Contents

Foreword

With *Getting Our Bodies Back*, the addictions/recovery field has grown a healthy body. We have observed Christine's development of the Moving Cycle over many years and celebrate the emergence of her book. This accessible and magically sensible approach springs directly from thousands of hours of witnessing people claim their full aliveness. This is the first comprehensive method that truly honors the intelligence and innate healing capacity of the whole body-mind. Christine lays out a map of this territory that is easy to follow and electrifying to use.

Christine founded and developed the somatic psychology program at Naropa Institute, where many of the strategies and practices described in this book were studied and refined. This program is one of the few places where students learn to utilize the power of deep witnessing and to follow the organic movement process while developing a rich inner life. One of Christine's great gifts is the skill of forming random events into comprehensible categories. The web she weaves from the seeming chaos of body phenomena is a breakthrough in treatment that will refresh and renew practitioners and curious people from many professions.

Getting Our Bodies Back is a guided tour of what Moshe Feldenkrais calls "the elusive obvious." It shows you how to befriend the disowned body you live in and move into wholeness.

The whole field of psychology needs this book and the wealth of healing it offers. Christine, in this book as in her life, is generous with herself, sharing her discoveries with transparency and humor. We predict this work will be required reading for anyone who wants to be truly effective and have a heart-centered humorous healing journey.

GAY and KATHLYN HENDRICKS

Getting Our Bodies Back

Introduction
Discovering the Source

When we are embodied, we become learners.
—RICHARD STROZZI HECKLER,
The Anatomy of Change

Some years ago after a spectacular binge, I finally grumped and whined my way into admitting I had an addictive relationship to sugar. I had all the typical signs: hiding it, sneaking it, being out of control with it, lying about it. A short while after this confession, on a trip to the local mall, I bought a large cookie to share with my four-year-old son. As we settled down to eat, my attention was drawn to him as he murmured contentedly, munched noisily, and consumed his half with delighted joy. I inhaled my half with obsessive greed, worrying about how fattening it was and wondering if anyone I knew was watching. The contrast in our experiences, given that it was the same cookie, shook me. I felt a stab in my heart as I realized that somewhere along the line I had lost the happy relationship with cookies that he still had. The difference between us in that moment seemed to be that he was awake and alive, while I was shut down and withdrawn.

I vowed to myself that from that moment on I would let myself eat as much sugar as I wanted, but only when I could stay "awake" and truly celebrate the experience as

much as my son had. My previous bouts with abstinence
had left me feeling deprived, empty, anxious, and just as
addicted as ever. I longed to practice what I saw in my
son—a physical aliveness and centeredness in the present
that seemed to elude me when it came to sugar—whether
I was actually eating it or not. What I subsequently discovered was that it was almost impossible for me to do this.
At the first sweet bite I would enter a state of oblivion, eat
quickly and furtively, and then feel miserable. In short, I
was not awake and alive, and this was not a pleasurable
experience. It felt more like a driven experience, with the
same familiar outcome of self-absorption and self-hatred.

As I stuck with my commitment to eat sugar only when
I could remain present, I occasionally stayed conscious for
a few seconds at a time as I nibbled, and I began to explore
this awakeness. In those brief moments, I could *see* the
cookie; I could luxuriate in its smell and texture; I could
savor the taste and truly treasure it. I was actually having
a rich sensory experience, albeit a fleeting one. I was
amazed to realize that I derived immense pleasure more
from the act of staying awake than from the actual eating
of the cookie. Sensation was wonderful! And as I continued to stay awake, I found that I didn't really want much
sugar. The experience of eating it while awake was so rich
and full that a very small amount was all it took to satisfy
me. If I monitored the pleasure, it began to taper off
quickly. If I stopped at that point, the taste of joy lingered
in my mouth. If I continued to eat, I began to feel slightly
sick. I found myself eating much less and enjoying it much
more. A little bit of something sweet once in a while was
enough to occasion great happiness. And my body told me
when to stop. This in itself, this feeling that my body was
choosing, making a clear yes or no statement, was quite

amazing. When I stayed awake in my body, I could feel the harmful effects of eating more than a bite or two. I could feel my blood sugar shift as I sensed the subtle signs in my body—a slight sweatiness, a higher heart rate, and a sick feeling in my stomach. I actually began to feel the difference between toxins and nourishers in my body—not just with sugar, but increasingly with all foods. I hadn't expected my body to wake up as a part of this process, and stumbling onto this result was astonishing. What I was discovering was the incredible power of self-regulation that is our birthright. This choosing power had been lost in the throes of the addiction.

This experiment worked because I had already exited my denial and had admitted that I was addicted. I had also committed myself to recovery by making my awakeness more important than the addiction. Sugar is not inherently poisonous—unlike nicotine, alcohol, and many other drugs, for which complete abstinence and detoxification is required before the work of recovery can proceed. But our bodies cannot discriminate between poison and nourishment, much less choose between them, until we are physically out from under the influence of the poison. The poison obscures our choosing power. Thus, people who have become addicted to powerful poisons may find that they must never again ingest even small amounts of them.

The benefits of my awakeness practice have been far-reaching. When I inhabit my body, I can self-regulate; I can judge for myself when a substance is toxic to me, when only small amounts of it are OK, or when it is a food, pleasant and nourishing. I can also know when things like behaviors, relationships, and thought patterns are toxic, neutral, or nourishing. I have only to tune in to myself to know, and from there I must go on to the next, even more challenging step: that of tolerating and even welcoming the joy and health that result from actually being in my body and consistently choosing nourishment.

This process can alter our very notion of what nourishment is. When we are addicted, we can never get enough of the thing we crave and our concept of nourishment can contract into a survival-based longing for *more* coupled with a primal experience of *not enough*. When we inhabit our bodies and reclaim self-regulation, we find that nourishment consists in having just enough of the right thing. Addiction interferes with our ability to sense what the right thing is. It also interferes with our ability to sense whether any nourishment (be it food, touch, attention, stimulation) is not enough, just right, or too much. When we get too much of anything, it becomes a poison. Even water and oxygen can kill us if we take in too much. When there is not enough, our lives are poisoned by the constant search for more.

I am a body-centered psychotherapist. Body-centered psychotherapy is a kind of clinical work that puts the body into action as a means of accessing repressed and fragmented parts of the self. It operates on the premise that sensation, breath, and movement are the body's form of speech, and that if we listen to this speech we can complete and release stored trauma, relearn how to feel excitement and pleasure, and engage in activities that nourish. This body speech often arises from our unconscious, or from parts of ourselves that have become fragmented and from which we have withdrawn. It can manifest as aches and pains, chronic health conditions, postural and gestural habits, or unusual sensations.

I first began working with addictions (in a way recognizable as such) in my private practice in 1984, a few years before my own nascent recovery. While still in the throes of my own sugar addiction, I was noticing certain physical behaviors in my clients that were both puzzling and difficult to watch. I was noticing what I came to call movement habits—mostly gestures and body tensions that a client exhibited when he or she became charged with feeling. These habits were usually small repeating movements, often of the hands or face, that had no functional or expressive use and that seemed to act like a sedative. It was common for me to catch these habits at pivotal points in a session, when key feelings or insights were emerging.

This pattern was particularly striking with one client whose mother had died of cancer when she was four. In our sessions she began to feel some of the unexpressed grief and loss of that experience. At those times her face would momentarily lose its usual mask of impassiveness and become transformed by an expression of sadness. She would then unconsciously rub her face with her hands, at which point the sad feeling would, coincidentally, be gone, and she would report feeling a bit lost. When I pointed out this gesture to her, I learned that she was totally unaware that she did it. She subsequently began to observe this habit in her daily life and found that she rubbed her face whenever she became uncomfortable with what she was feeling.

Instead of trying to stop the pattern, we went into it consciously. She began to rub her face purposely, allowing the gesture to develop in whatever way it wanted to go. The face-rubbing got more intense as she was able to recall a specific memory of her father, after her mother's funeral, literally telling her to "wipe that look off" her face, to be a good girl, not to cry, to forget about it. As she rubbed more vigorously, she was able to contact and express the rage she felt at not being allowed to cry for her mother. This cleared the way for her to do the long-postponed grieving, which manifested in her weeping with her face in her hands for two whole sessions. After these sessions she off-handedly reported a marked decrease in her craving for cigarettes.

I uncovered such subtle body behaviors in myself as well as in my clients. I welcomed my own physical habits like old friends, comfortable and familiar, who gave me a continuing sense of self-identity and who kept my uncomfortable feelings at bay. After all, picking at my fingernails when I was nervous was a regular and comfortable part of who I was.

I witnessed nearly all my clients withdrawing their awareness from their bodies and performing habitual behaviors when under stress, whether they were dealing with identifiable addictions or not. I also bemusedly found that clients were very predictable in their use of these habits. I could predict when one of my clients would rub his chin. It would happen whenever he talked about his relationship with his father. With another client, I knew that whenever she began to feel angry, she would pull on her hair. Observations like these are common among movement therapists and even many verbal therapists, yet identifying the behaviors and treating them as roots of the addictive process is not.

I woke up to the knowledge that our naturally expressive, creative, voluptuous bodies can be held captive in any addictive process, while we remain only marginally aware of it. This revelation—that addiction involves leaving our bodies in a way that takes away self-awareness, helping us flee from what we are experiencing—was a surprise. I had always assumed that all body expression was an act of consciousness emerging. In a sense this was true, but I was now observing a category of movement that I had not previously known—movement that was neither functional nor expressive, but regressive. I discovered that we can be addicted to our own body habits as ways to mitigate pain and seek euphoria just as we take substances or engage in numbing behaviors that do the same thing. Whenever the going gets too rough, we need to leave our bodies in order to lessen the intensity of what we are feeling.

This book is the result of the reading, clinical observations, and therapeutic trials that resulted from these early experiences. It calls for the development of a new definition of addiction that includes our understanding of the body's role in reclaiming our wholeness and joy, that outlines the nature of addiction in our physical behavior, and that suggests new treatment methods.

The addictions recovery movement has produced an extensive body of valuable writing, particularly in the last ten years. The field has attained a level of clinical and theoretical refinement on a par with that of classical psychology. The addictions recovery movement was born out of necessity, and has been crafted by those who needed it most. This gives it a unique, earthy quality that, because it is so practical, has made it so highly valuable to so many. What is the next level of development for this field? I believe it lies in the area of recovering our bodies, and working with addiction's deepest root—physical desensitization and habituation.

Most addicted people will tell you that they hate their body, that they mistrust it, or that they have very little sense of it. This is because their bodies have literally stored the cast-off pain of early trauma and abuse, like a garbage dump for the disowned pieces of their lives. Who wants to live in a garbage dump? For those who do, coming back into their bodies represents only a reawakening of feelings of shame, wrongness, or abandonment. In fact, most of us feel this about our bodies to some extent. This idea was never more eloquently put than by the television star Roseanne, who, in *People* magazine in October 1991, went public with her memories of severe child abuse:

> I have lived the majority of my life in a flesh prison that I was always trying to blow up, break out of, whittle away. I tortured my body, smoking five packs of cigarettes a day and indulging in drug, alcohol and food abuse that had me weighing either a hundred or two hundred pounds. I was scratching and tearing at my body—mutilating myself. It was as if punishing my body would turn me into an angel of some sort, an angel that could transcend my body—a body I hated because it was the holder of the truth, the secret.

We are conceived and born with these incredibly soft, juicy, and pliant containers we call bodies. We experience ourselves and the world through them. We shape ourselves through bodily experiences as we grow. All the joy and pain and minute mundane happenings that life presents us are processed and expressed through our bodies. If we experience wounding that is never resolved, that trauma impacts on our physical tissues, and our body will try its best to cope by whatever means it knows. If the trauma is consistent and unrelenting, our physical coping becomes consistent and unrelenting, and body addiction is born: our body learns strategies that keep us alive, even if it means cutting off the aliveness of nonessential parts. Addiction is the emotional and psychic equivalent of frostbite—in the face of it we withdraw aliveness from nonessential, peripheral things like our own creativity and happiness in order to save the core, and we do this in our body, first and foremost. Curiously enough, it is through reclaiming our body that these and all our addictions can be treated. This book is about the physical journey into and out of the life crisis and life opportunity of addiction.

Part One looks at the developmental process of addiction in the body: the reasons we turn to movement as an escape from direct experience, the stages of the addictive process in the body, and the relationship of movement addictions to the more vivid and identified addictions of substance abuse, process abuse, and codependency.

Part Two demonstrates how movement and body-centered approaches can be used to reverse the addictive process and help us reclaim our genuineness and vitality. Its premise is that any recovery is incomplete until we reinhabit and enjoy being in our bodies. Many recovering people achieve the astounding accomplishment of avoiding the frostbite response to life. Part Two is about extending our experience of recovery so that it is not just the absence of disease symptoms, but a gutsy, full-bodied, vibrant celebration of life, an actual experience of pleasure in the events of life, a rejoicing in being here that makes us all poets and dancers, lovers and painters, humanitarians of the highest order. Diane Ackerman understood this well when she wrote in her book *A Natural History of the Senses:*

> We like to think that we are finely evolved creatures, in suit-and-tie or pantyhose-and-chemise, who live many millennia and mental detours away from the cave, but that's not something our bodies are convinced of. We may have the luxury of being at the top of the food chain, but our adrenaline still rushes when we encounter real or imagi-

nary predators. . . . We still create works of art to enhance
our senses and add even more sensations to the brimming
world, so that we can utterly luxuriate in the spectacles of
life. We still ache fiercely with love, lust, loyalty, and pas-
sion. And we still perceive the world, in all its gushing
beauty and terror, right on our pulses. There is no other
way. To begin to understand the gorgeous fever that is consciousness, we must try to understand the senses . . . and
what they can teach us about the ravishing world we have
the privilege to inhabit (1990, xix).

This book is about using a body-centered paradigm—or
somatic psychology, as I will also call it—to transform a
raging disease into a gorgeous fever through reinhabiting
our bodies. Through this transformation our lives can explode with meaning, purpose, and grace.

Part One

Reembodying Our Concepts

1

It's All in Your Body

He who feels it, knows it more.
—BOB MARLEY

What is somatic psychology? *Soma* simply means "body." *Psyche* refers to the mind. Somatic psychology, then, is the study of the body-mind connection. It draws upon philosophy, medicine, and other sciences in an attempt to unify human beings into an organic whole for the purpose of healing and transformation. In a sense, we could say that somatic psychology seeks a unified field theory of human nature. This book paints a view of somatic psychology in broad strokes, based on the following basic premises.

1. *Any event that occurs—whether physical, emotional, cognitive, or spiritual—impacts our whole being.* Our experience of an event must come through the sensory systems permeating our flesh—through a pulsing network of nerves—in order to register in the mind. Our bodies must be in a certain state of alertness to be able even to think. And the only way that the mind is made real is through the actions of the body in which it is imbedded. Our response to events changes the body's physical structure as well as emotions and thoughts: anger registers in the jaw, sadness in the chest. Even thinking can be associated with a characteristic look on the face or a small hand gesture.

Our body/mind is a feedback loop or a continuum rather than two separate and (ideally) cooperative systems. Healthy functioning is a physical as well as an emotional and cognitive experience, and dysfunction in any part of the body-mind continuum will effect the whole system.

2. *As humans we are energy systems.* We both take in and put out energy in order to live, and that energy exchange determines our identity and our behavior. Energy can be seen as the equivalent of personality. From a somatic perspective, we look at how energy from the environment—everything from food to conversation—is absorbed into people, how it is processed by them, and how they express it back out. Events stimulate energy flow in us. This energy is then interpreted through its impact on the shape and density of our physical structure. If I have been criticized, I will shrink in my chest area. If I shrink in my chest area, I am likely to interpret people's words as criticism. This energy is then discharged into the environment in the form of behavior, such as being verbally defensive, or passive, or withdrawn. Energy is often overbound or underbound in the body, as a result of consistently using either contraction or collapse as a defense strategy.

3. *Our energy is so basic a life function that it cannot be bad.* Much of our suffering is a result of being punished for having our energy. Wilhelm Reich believed that modern society was a major repressive force that squelched and perverted our core energies, and that this repression was the basis for all illness. This view contrasts with Sigmund Freud's concept of the libido, which he saw as a form of primitive, unsocialized energy in us that must be reined in and controlled for society to operate. But according to our premise, to judge any of our energy to be out of control and potentially dangerous creates a self-fulfilling proph-

ecy—whatever energy we hate or fear *will* become distorted and wounded by not being felt or expressed normally.

4. *We are organized around an energy loop of feeling and expressing.* Feeling is generally equated with sensation and with the pulsatory flow of energy in the body. It occurs inside our bodies, and is the raw data from which we learn to label our emotions, moods, and states. Our ability to stay receptive to sensation and energy in an unconditional manner is a prime component of healthy functioning. Many body-centered therapists work to reclaim sensation and energy pulsation by having clients practice tracking and validating their sensory awareness (Gendlin 1978; Hanna 1987). In a sense, it is Freud's free association on a bodily level.

Expression is another prime component of healthy functioning. We can express ourselves only through our bodies, whether by speech or gesture. We look for expression that accurately communicates our inner experience. If we hold our expressions in, we are called rigid, uptight, or withdrawn, and if we overexpress, we are thought to be hysterical, dramatic, or out of control.

5. *Our bodies love to move and must move.* Movement is the way we define life—when our heart beats, lungs pulse, brain waves, we are alive; in the absence of movement we become inanimate or dead. All body movements can be seen as vibratory or pulsatory phenomena on a continuum from gross and slow (physical progress through space) to midlevel (fluids coursing in the body, gestures, emotional flutters) to fine and fast (ion exchange, electrical impulses). The expansion and contraction of the pulsatory process is life at its primal best—breathing in and out, the squeezing and relaxing alternations in digestion, and the

heart swelling with blood, then compressing it out. The process is echoed macrocosmically in the pulsating nature of the universe, and microcosmically in the quivering of the fertilized egg. In its simplest form, somatic diagnosis is an assessment of where the person is experiencing the pulsating movement of life in his or her body and where he or she is not.

6. *When movement is held back, energy/life flow is impeded, and we become sick. When movement is rushed, energy/life flow is distorted, and we become sick.* This sickness manifests in our entire being: in our physical bodies, through areas of tension and blockage, or hyperactivity; in our emotions, as withdrawal from feeling and expressing, or outbursts or inappropriate feeling; in our cognitive processes, as fixed views or runaway obsessive thinking; and in our spiritual lives, as a sense of meaninglessness and lack of connection. Suffering originates when we try to grasp and hold still or accelerate into fight-or-flight patterns rather than experience movement that dances with what is occurring.

7. *The body is a symbol for all experience.* This is illustrated in the ways we use language. Saying that someone is a pain in the neck may really reflect how we tense up in their presence. Getting an ulcer says something about one's abdominal energy flow. Dreaming about having no legs is a statement about standing and grounding. When we trust our somatic symptoms we can listen to our words, images, and dreams about the body to assess how we view and organize our experience. We know that the body is constantly speaking to us in the language of sensation, and that this speech, though not in words, is a vital and rich source of information and intuition.

Given these premises, we can begin to look at addiction in a new light. *Addiction* comes from the Latin word meaning "devoted habits." From a somatic perspective, then, addiction can be anything our bodies do habitually. T. C. Schneirla (1959) pointed out that animals at all levels of the evolutionary scale have innate mechanisms of approach and withdrawal. These basic mechanisms are at the root of all motivational behavior. He found that addiction had to do with our motivation to approach. He believed that an addictive substance is anything that, when administered, will produce forward locomotion, or moving toward something. It appears that substances induce forward locomotion by activating dopamine circuitry in the medial forebrain bundle, the area of the brain involved in reward. Reward will elicit approach behaviors. In the case of food, an animal will approach the food. In the case of centrally administered brain stimulation, the animal merely moves forward, apparently approaching the most salient objects in the environment.

This theory says that in addiction our brain is programmed to compel us to reach for what rewarded it. In this sense, addiction is a programmed movement behavior of approach. The beauty of this theory is that it is currently the only one that can encompass the extremely variable workings of many diverse addictive substances as well as behaviors such as gambling and sex. We will compulsively move our body toward whatever we have conditioned ourselves to associate with reward. It is my belief that addiction is also a simultaneous motivational behavior of withdrawal. While we approach reward, we also flee pain.

Alcoholics Anonymous, which was founded before the Second World War, was the first system to address addic-

tion as a process of simultaneous approach and withdrawal. With the advent of AA, which set many thousands
of addicts on a path of recovery, the prevailing view of
alcoholism as a character weakness began to evaporate. In
1962 the American Medical Association declared alcoholism a disease and stated that it should be treated as such.
The disease model of alcoholism heralded a crucial stage
in the field's evolution, as it allowed treatment to be more
focused and effective. The twelve-step program was instituted in almost every treatment center, and the recovery
rate for this disease began to improve dramatically.

Part of working the twelve-step program has to do with
sharing one's recovery with others. I believe it is partly
from the influence of step twelve that the large number of
popular books and articles on dependency and recovery
have arisen: recovering addicts began to write, to share the
fruits of their recovery journey. Another reason this area in
the literature became so influential is that what was being
written seemed to enrich and explain so much about vast
related areas of psychological theory. Suddenly we were
turning to recovering addicts to explain dysfunctional
family systems. We turned to the addictions field to study
deeply the phenomenon of the inner child. We learned
from addicts the different family roles assigned to children
that molded them into dysfunctional adults.

What occurred in this breakthrough time, beginning
around 1980, was that we began to see that there are many
types of addiction besides chemical ones, such as addictions to sex, tobacco, money, work, food, or gambling;
that more people are addicted than was previously
thought—when we expand our definition of addiction, we
see that most of us fall into it—and that addiction is rooted
in a widespread dysfunctional family system, which has

discernible rules that keep its members from getting their needs met.

From this viewpoint, addiction is not necessarily the stuff of drunks and druggies; it is simply a very human movement, a consistent habit of withdrawing from ourselves. At the same time, it is an automatic reaching for something that is *not* ourselves. In some cases this can be life threatening, though in most cases it simply washes away the vibrant color in life, dampens the song of it, turns our ecstatic dance into a shuffle. Addiction looms for most of us not as a depraved monster but as a failure of creativity, a fear of "following our bliss," as Joseph Campbell put it.

As a body-centered psychotherapist, it is interesting and shocking for me to note that there is, in all the voluminous literature on this subject, a dearth of information on the body in addiction or recovery. There are few books or articles on it, and only a few of the major authors do anything more than mention it in passing. Other than knowing the physiological processes and results of addiction, few authors seem to know or care that addiction is housed in and carried out in a body, and that recovery must occur within it. This simple truth is neglected, I believe, for two reasons. The first is that the society at large is inexperienced with this idea; we still tend to see the body as a utilitarian tool. The second is that addiction is an act of poisoning a body we have come to hate because it is in our bodies that we experience pain, particularly the pain of need deprivation. And we tend to avoid writing about subjects we hate.

The standard joke in the addictions recovery field is that you will see more cigarettes, coffee, and donuts at an AA meeting than anywhere else. Many AA members are working so hard to abstain from drinking or drug use that these other more "minor" addictions seem relatively harmless. But engaging in these death-affirming addictions serves to cut off the body's pain messages almost as effectively as drinking does. And when you can't hear your body, you don't include it in the equation of recovery—and most authors have not.

Within this paucity of awareness, a few islands of awakeness occur. Charles Whitfield (1987) acknowledges that we have a basic need for things like touching and skin contact, and that interfering with this need can cause addiction. Anne Wilson-Schaef (1988) mentions that physical illness is a characteristic of codependence. Marion Woodman wrote a section on the body as a sacred vessel in her book *Addiction to Perfection* (1982). In it she advocates listening to the messages from our bodies (sensations, dream imagery) as an adjunctive path to recovery. John Bradshaw (1990) recommends activities that physically feel good, and are nourishing for the body, as a method for reclaiming the inner child.

While these authors grasp the involvement of the body in some aspect of recovery, no one has put forth a systematic theory of the body's role in the etiology, development, and course of addiction. Without such a theory to operate from, any mention of the body in recovery will remain a note in passing, and the addictions we all deal with will be that much harder to face.

What a body-centered approach can do is decognify healing and transformation. When we put most of our attention on our concepts of self, on knowing who we are, we miss the vital nourishment of directly experiencing the world without perceptual and belief-system filters. Our happiness lies in our ability to experience life directly and to the hilt. Knowing *who* we are, in this light, can be a

vastly overrated act. Knowing who we are gives us all sorts
of ideas or stories to tell. I am a woman, a mother, a
teacher, a psychotherapist. While these are all accurate labels, do they really encompass me? Like a compass, do
they locate me for myself and for others? Ideas may or
may not be accurate; they are certainly shaped by what
we have been told about ourselves and by our needs for
approval and attention. Knowing who we are provides a
view that can dictate how we see the world and how we
act in it. It gives us a box to live in.

It is the act of locating ourselves, of saying "Here I am,
in the here and now!" that gives our lives its luminescence
and beauty. When we know *where* we are, we can move
in any direction life takes us. Locating myself in space im-
beds me in my environment, like having a compass. It is
delightful to sit gazing out the window, only to catch ourselves and say, "Oh, I was a million miles away!" We then
have an opportunity to return home. Where is home? The
only home we will have for our whole lives, twenty-four
hours a day, is our bodies. Being a million miles away in
our thoughts may be a pleasant diversion, but it can allow
us to miss a beautiful sunset, or the light in our children's
eyes.

Now is the only time we are present and accounted for.
When our thoughts go into the future or into the past, we
can plan, remember, or compare. But the only time we can
act is now. Being in the present moment creates direct experience. Direct experience puts us in touch with our aliveness, with the accurate perception of being in the world
and of the world. Being in the here and now awakens us
to knowledge of the vibrant, pulsing body in which we live
and move.

Most traditional cultures use legends, myths, and stories

to define and locate themselves. One archetypal story form is the hero's, or heroine's, journey. On the surface of this story, the heroine faces a crisis in her own land, some threat to the kingdom. She must go on a journey to find the solution to this danger. In the course of her travels, she is transformed by this quest and comes home with new skills and understandings that save the kingdom. Looking at the inner landscape of the heroine's journey we can recognize the search for our deepest self, our essence. This is done by the hero or heroine often without a map. Like the hero, we too long to know where we are in relation to the world around us, and how we may relate to others in this world in a satisfying way. Questions arise: What are the sources of nourishment that we can take along the road to sustain us? Where and what is the road that will take us there? What mode of transportation do we use?

The following chapters look at our innate resources for the journey of locating ourselves, how we learn to abandon them—and how we can learn to reclaim them. These chapters will help us construct a road map for the quest. They also provide a look at the road home, supplying a map and compass for again locating our birthright of direct experience, of vital aliveness.

2

Jumping Ship
The Body's Role in Addiction

You do not have to be good.
You do not have to walk on your knees
for a hundred miles through the desert, repenting.
You only have to let the soft animal of your body
love what it loves. . . .
—MARY OLIVER, *"Wild Geese"*

Addiction is not so much substance use or a behavioral process as it is a movement away from our direct body experience of the real world. Withdrawing from our bodies is the beginning of any addictive behavior. It is the making of the internal statement, "This experience is too much, so I am leaving my body right now." When we vacate our bodies, we get away from any sensations, emotions, and mental states that we find threatening. We get out of touch with ourselves in order to avoid directly experiencing what is going on. Addiction is an out-of-body experience, a pulling the plug on our connection to ourselves and the world.

We all dissociate, whether for a moment as we look out a car window, or for days on an alcoholic binge. The process of "checking out" probably evolved as soon as human beings had enough spare neurons to pull it off. We can use mild dissociation as a way to rest, as we do when sitting in front of the TV in a mild trance. I notice that I dissociate most frequently when I am in an intense work period. I also notice that dissociating rests my mind but not my body. The more I do it, the more I want to do it. It becomes addictive, and the more I do it, the less satisfied and refreshed I feel.

Freud pioneered a technique called free association, an exercise in which the mind is relaxed, not focusing on anything in particular, and thoughts are allowed to arise spontaneously, without the usual filters of social appropriateness, common sense, or practicality. The technique was used by artists and writers such as Virginia Woolf, whose experiments with stream-of-consciousness writing echoed it. Both Freud and the modern artists noticed that free-associating gave access to the most authentic, creative, elemental aspects of self and of human existence. Free association is the formal application of the state I call *active rest*. This is the state that echoes in our body when we are doing some easy, relatively goalless activity. I like to take walks, my father likes to work on antique cars, a friend of mine sews—each of these activities leads us to a state of active rest. Some forms of play can also be an active rest, a kind of physical free association. Play is one of the few activities we do solely for the sake of doing it. Meditation is also a kind of active resting—staying alert while we calm body and mind.

Active resting gets lost in a society that values work and productivity over happiness and self-realization. When we define ourselves in terms of our jobs and careers, we develop a work-work-work-collapse pattern. Does this sound familiar? How many times have I worked a twelve-hour day and then come home and felt that all I could do was sit in front of the TV and eat popcorn? Dissociating becomes a seductive alternative to active rest.

Active resting involves a conjoining of body and mind. In active rest we relax our thoughts and we allow our bodies to stay awake. Our senses stay alert and can even become heightened. We allow ourselves to notice things we may have passed by as we worked—the smell of an apple, the feeling of the muscles in our back, the vividness of a sunset—and in doing so we reclaim our connection to ourselves and our world. This reconnection can be deeply refreshing after a period of narrow attentional focus. In this way we can shift our sequence into a work-rest-work-rest mode, one which leaves us at the end of the day feeling satisfied and alive.

I read recently that we modern human types work longer and harder than our Neanderthal ancestors and than most indigenous hunter-gatherer cultures by a full eight to ten hours per week. In these societies, work is combined with visiting, teaching, and play. There is little separation between the time and place of work and the time and place of rest. Though most of us do not live this way, we can reclaim the work–active rest–work–active rest mode. We can use sleep as our deep resting and employ our other waking hours with refreshing and nourishing and reconnecting activities. We can recover ourselves, so that dissociation is replaced by free association.

Getting in the Habit

When we abandon active rest, when we focus narrowly on one activity for long periods of time, or when we feel consistently powerless in the face of repeated events, we compel ourselves to dissociate. We enter a state of need deprivation, at the same time creating a response that does nothing to fill our needs, but merely dampens our perception that we are in need. And to dissociate we must leave our bodies. The abandonment of our body forms the root of addiction. In this sense, the addictive process can begin as soon as we learn to move our bodies. Our first and most basic needs are physical, and as infants our first ability to respond and make our needs known is through our body and its movement. As babies we cry, squirm, nuzzle, root, bang our fists, and make other movements to make our needs known. This body language is interpreted by our parents so that they can take care of our needs. If, however, we have been born to parents and caregivers who have not had their own needs met, these movements will be ignored or responded to chaotically or inappropriately. When this occurs, we learn that what we need is not there, will not come, and so we may feel the constant ache and unresolvable pain of need deprivation.

This feeling can be quite overwhelming, and quite physical. It can also teach us that our bodies are bad or unimportant, that they are parts of us that irritate or confuse our parents and get us no results. This kind of experience cannot be tolerated for long. We want to "kill the messenger," our body. It is here, within the soft body of the young child, where the first addictions are born.

I had one client who, as a small child, was locked in a closet whenever she cried or got upset. In addition to the intense trauma this act created, it also deprived her of her need to feel safe, loved, and cared for. In the closet, she would hug her knees and rock back and forth, crooning nonsense songs to herself so she wouldn't hear any frightening sounds. She also reported that as a child in that closet she would "visit heaven," (leave her body) until her mother came and let her out. She could dissociate well enough that she could literally feel herself hovering over her body, looking down on it. As an adult, she would assume this fetal posture whenever she was under stress. And at such times she reported not being able to feel anything. This was a reenactment of an early survival strategy. Her ability to withdraw from her body, which had been under overwhelming stress that she could do nothing to assuage, may have saved her life.

A bulimic client, in the face of her father's sexual abuse of her, would "visit the angels." As an adult, visiting the angels became an automatic and far too frequent occurrence, interfering with her ability to form relationships.

It is in response to experiences that we are helpless to prevent that we first leave our bodies in ways like the above clients of mine did. We may report simply feeling detached, numb, or blank. We are aware only of thinking, and thinking need not occur in the real world, the one where we may be having a hard time—and that can seem a great advantage. In order to get away from real pain, we have to withdraw from our awareness of these bodies that live in the real world and register everything that happens in it. Our bodies are clever. Like children in a fairy tale, they leave a trail of bread crumbs to help them find their way back out of the dark forest. Our bodies use movement habits to mark the spot where we check out. Like a bread crumb trail, these gestures enable us to trace our way home.

This process was illustrated by a client who was trying to give up smoking. He began to show me how much fun it was to make the hand gestures of smoking, laughing as he pantomimed bringing the cigarette to his lips, sucking on it, using it to make social gestures. When I asked him

to close his eyes and stay with the feelings that came up
with the gestures, he gradually became sad, began to rub
his lips lightly with his fingertips, and then began to cry
softly, saying quietly, "No one ever kissed or hugged me."

The body movements we develop when we are young
are the modus operandi of dissociating. Typical movement
habits are chewing on fingers; sucking on body parts; persistent rubbing, picking, or hitting body parts; or autistic
gestures. It is important to note that all children make such
movements to some degree as part of their development. It
is when these movements become repetitive substitutes for
interaction with the world that they can be seen as addictive. These addictive body movements become neurologi-
cally and psychologically habituated. They become automatic and unconscious. As growing children we can numb
out in small ways many, many times a day, using our bodies like addictive substances, taking away pain and substi-
tuting obliviousness whenever we feel stressed. In adult-
hood our bread crumb trails evolve into the way we cock
our head, a habit of pursing our lips, a rubbing together of
our thumb and forefinger—all easy, all automatic, all no
big deal.

Needs start from conception and are biologically based.
The basic needs for food, protection, warmth, and acceptance begin in the womb. These needs can be interfered
with by the mother's actions and her own addictive patterns so that the experience of not being adequately cared
for can begin before birth. When need deprivation starts
this early in development, the toxic imprint can perma-
nently damage the psyche and body of the child. As adults,
people who have suffered this way are often so self-
destructive and/or suicidal that they cannot function.

This point was brought home to me when I worked with

a suicidal client who had difficulty sustaining relationships. She often said that her body felt poisoned and bad. She had recurring fantasies about knifing herself in the abdomen. The only way she could deal with feeling upset was to hit herself in the umbilical region with her fist. When we explored her history, she reported that her mother was an alcoholic and had been one since before her birth. For months in utero, her developing body was fed alcohol via the umbilical cord, and there was no way to prevent it from flooding her body. We now realize that alcohol is poisonous to fetuses, but my client had not linked her prenatal history to her current distress. When she was able to acknowledge her fetal alcohol syndrome, she was able to transform her self-destructive hitting movements into cathartic vomiting and screaming. From there she began to rebuild a self-concept that included knowing that she was a survivor and not a person who deserved her mysterious pain.

Most of us did not suffer to this degree. Most of us had comparatively safe childhoods. Our habits of dissociating are usually milder ones and are often socially acceptable. In dissociating with the TV or with food or with two glasses of wine, we simply shave off a bit of aliveness, eliminate some of the juiciness from our lives. We pay our bills, we go skiing, we laugh with our friends. And it may only be in rare quiet moments that we question what these behaviors are all about.

The Addictive Spiral

The process and practice of addiction, whether it be to a drug or to a recurrent thought, is illustrated in what I call the Addictive Spiral. The spiral begins with *intolerable ex-*

perience. This is some experience that is so painful or pleasurable or otherwise overwhelming that it is perceived as threatening to our physical, emotional, or psychic survival. Examples of this kind of trauma are physical or sexual abuse, psychological abuse, abandonment, a history of disapproval at being happy or excited, or a feeling of being unwanted. We can also learn that pleasure is intolerable. My own earliest memory is from age three. I was riding my tricycle down the hill in front of my house, and I got going so fast that my feet couldn't stay on the spinning pedals. I extended my feet out and shrieked with joy at the speed, the thrill, the fun of it. As I approached the bottom of the hill, I hit a brick sitting on the pavement, and the sudden deceleration crashed me onto my face, breaking my nose. I think that was the moment I decided that great pleasure was dangerous, particularly physical fun. As a growing child and young adult, I would never do anything full out physically, and whenever an opportunity to do so arose, my friends would report that I would make a characteristic rubbing gesture with my finger on the side of my nose.

Intolerable experience can also happen when we become so habituated to narrowly focusing on work or so unused to active rest that a real juicy experience is threatening simply by contrast. The intolerable experience stimulates a fight-or-flight reaction, making the body tense, agitated, and eager to do something to relieve the situation.

Because this state cannot be tolerated and maintained for long, we construct *control* in the next stage of the spiral. In order to accomplish control, we withdraw self-awareness from the body. We avoid thinking about how we feel, and we avoid feelings and body sensations that may prolong the upset. This is accomplished cognitively by denial and physically by numbing or depressing our senses. As I have said before, physical sensations, touch, taste, hearing, vision, smell, are the raw material for emotions. Without them, emotions cannot get started. If we can desensitize the basic sensations, we can cut off the feelings. However, the raw data of sensation remains there, buried. Freud called this process sublimation: a pushing down of the feeling below the level of conscious awareness, to be stored in the unconscious. Our unconscious doesn't like to be used as a storage dump in this way (it has other more important things to do), and it will assert itself through dreams, behavior slips, fantasies, and other behaviors in order to alert us to the existence of these refugee emotions. One favorite way we deal with our unconscious efforts to feel unwanted feelings is to project the feelings out onto others. "Everyone else is angry, not me"; or "I'm not sad, the sad movie just made me cry."

Another favorite control mechanism for dealing with sublimation is denial. As our bodies desensitize, our minds must justify the process and agree with what we are doing. Denial is the mental equivalent of desensitization. It is saying something is not there in order to make it not be there. Denial is so common in addicted people that it is one of the primary means used to diagnose addiction.

Patterned movement and body gestures are our first attempts at denial and desensitization. They literally distract us from unwanted sensation by creating self-soothing alternatives. The phenomenon of control has been well documented by traditional addictions theory but with no awareness of the physical component of control that goes hand-in-hand with it. Our bodies must tense, shut down, and provide distracting alternatives in order to accomplish control in our thoughts and behavior.

Control is very costly; it takes a lot of energy to maintain. It uses many of our personal resources to monitor and select the experiences and feelings that are acceptable or unacceptable. The cost is our aliveness. Whenever we control our experience, we sacrifice a measure of vitality. Most of my clients come into therapy wanting to get rid of certain feelings and only experience certain other, better ones. While it makes sense to want to feel good, doing it through control ultimately fails. It takes a while for many clients to realize this: that the strain and fatigue of control is actually causing their suffering, not the feelings they were trying to select and discard.

When we are not feeling, sensing, or perceiving optimally, our relationships with both our inner self and with others become distorted. We are not perceiving accurately but through a filter of *shoulds, can'ts,* and *better nots.* Even though we deny and desensitize, our unfinished feelings are still there, deeply buried. We come to hate these feelings and to consider ourselves and others wrong, unlovable, or even disgusting for having them. The resulting feelings of shame herald the next phase of the addictive spiral: *rejection.*

Two kinds of feelings or experiences must be rejected in order to pull off an addictive process. The first is any feeling or thought that was considered intolerable by our family of origin. If as a child our anger threatens the working of the family system, our membership in the family will be in peril until we rid ourselves of it. Either the feeling goes or we go. For children, this leaves little choice: the feeling goes. And along with it goes a part of our self. In order to get rid of the feeling, we must reject it, making it "wrong." After all, our family seems to think it is bad, so we become a bad girl or a bad boy if we are caught with that feeling.

But when we discover that the feeling doesn't entirely go away, we have to be vigilant in continuously blocking it. One favorite technique for doing this is to internalize the family's strategy and to hate and reject the feeling. We take over the job of hating the angry feeling so that we don't have to experience the more frightening threat of our family's intolerance of it. We thus become self-hating in order to survive.

The second thing we must reject is any experience that threatens our self-hatred. Because self-hatred becomes crucial for survival, we must work to maintain it. One way to do this is to ignore or deny anything that affirms our aliveness. I have seen my clients go to amazing lengths to dismiss compliments, humor, sexuality, joy, and excitement. I have found myself doing it, for that matter. I have on several occasions gotten so scared of relationships that were going well that I unconsciously arranged to end them.

Self-affirmation and humor are such important signs of aliveness that I use them to diagnose clients caught in an addictive process: the inability to tolerate humor and the unwillingness to be affirmed in one's inherent goodness are telltale signs of addiction.

Another marvelous way to ensure the continuation of self-hatred is to intentionally or seemingly unintentionally "mess up." If we break our promises, for example, we can even get other people to reject us, thus reaffirming our inherent wrongness. In this rejection we can also lose our integrity and our joy in being responsible—as the shame and self-hatred become more important than keeping agreements. When keeping our promises generates feelings we don't want to feel—like satisfaction and affirmation—it becomes easier to simply not show up for appointments, not to tell the truth, not to respect others' rights or property. Unfortunately, the side effect of this rejection strategy is an increase in our self-hatred.

All this rejection results in a constriction of experience that makes the world look black and white to us—not only in the sense that the world loses its rich colors, but that we begin to think dualistically, assigning everything to categories as simple as black or white. We start to ignore random magnificence. A good example of this tendency is found in a statement of James Watt, Ronald Reagan's Secretary of the Interior, who said, "When you've seen one tree, you've seen them all." We focus on our body and our world as an object to be exploited (Watt, when shown a panoramic view of a forest, said, "Why aren't we cutting these down? That's a lot of wood going to waste"). In a black-and-white world, direct experiences are rare, and our ability to connect with our essence is marginalized.

The last phase of the addictions spiral has to do with the domino effect brought on by marginal experiencing: Because we exert so much energy on controlling and re-jecting our "wrong" experiences, we have fewer resources available that enable us to tolerate *any* experience. A lot of our time and energy goes into maintaining a defensive wall against an unacceptable body, which houses shameful thoughts and forbidden feelings and sensations. We have to get relief from the constant cost of control and shame. We commit ourselves to the very process of staying away from directly experiencing the world: we get drunk, high, binged out. We come to prefer oblivion, where there is less chance for pain, and less effort required to monitor which experiences are OK to have and which aren't. Substance abuse is so compelling because it temporarily lowers the cost of controlling our experience, because it takes over and runs our experience for us. We are let off the hook for a while. Movement addictions do this to a lesser extent than substances, which grab our consciousness and forcibly alter it. Substances give us a break from being in control, and they give us the illusion that we are being taken care of. Addiction puts a wide-screen TV into our prison cell, keeping us occupied with some entertaining movie while we serve out our sentence of self-hatred. In the Addictive Spiral this is called *desynchronization.*

Desynchronization means being out of step or out of time. In addiction, we opt to be out of step with our inner experience, which then results in a dysfunctional relationship with the outer world. If we cut off parts of our inner knowing, we cannot accurately read what is occurring in the world. We must isolate ourselves from the nourishment that the world can give us in order to maintain our self-hatred. We imagine that the whole world is like our family, disapproving or disallowing certain parts of us. This view is necessary for the preservation of our self-hatred. Assuming that our world is like our family of origin, we form core beliefs that support this. "It's a cruel world out there." "Do it to them before they do it to you." "Life's a bitch and then you die."

Our bodies assume physical stances to affirm and protect this desynchronization. We deflate our chest or lift our chin or raise our shoulders to anticipate the way we assume we will be treated. We dig in our heels, furrow our brow, or slump our torso to give everyone clues as to how we want to be treated. We choreograph a physical persona to relate with the world, while we bury our essence beneath it. These physical posturings keep the whole system going. We especially need to administer them to ourselves in times of stress, or when our act is threatened.

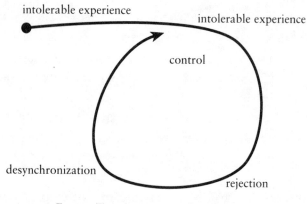

FIG. 1. THE ADDICTIVE SPIRAL

Figure 1 illustrates the Addictive Spiral. It begins with consistent intolerable experience, either pleasurable or painful. We then exert control to reject overwhelming feeling responses. We shape our body into a form that is acceptable, even though it can be like fitting a square peg into a round hole. This rejection causes us to lose touch with our essential selves and the mundane and glorious real world. We become desynchronous with both, our ill-fitting bodysuits disallowing an accurate relationship to both ourselves and our environment. This desynchroniza tion causes us to experience and behave inappropriately, resulting in further intolerable experience. The cycle continues.

The Addictive Spiral requires us to desensitize our bodies, to sublimate our natural desires, to deny our feelings, and to project all this onto others. This process involves lying. The fundamental act of saying, "This feeling I'm having is not mine" is a lie. We become our own Judas, betraying our whole self and committing ourselves to fragmentation. This lessens our integrity, because we cannot be responsible for what we have denied. We lose our ability to respond. We cannot trust ourselves or others. And this process constructs the beams and rafters of the house of our self-hatred. When we enter desynchronization, we cannot receive nourishment and support from the environment because we are out of synch with it. We feel sick, physically, emotionally, or spiritually, and our deficit of nourishment can give rise to a feeling of lack and scarcity, of fearful thinking and feeling. In order to control the fear we practice our addiction. Coming off the addiction will cause further fearful intolerable experiences.

Addictions can arise from repeated intolerable experiences of not getting our needs met, or from being punished for feeling pleasure at need gratification, or from consistently working without resting. Unmet needs are experienced in the body as an unbounded sense of lack or longing that can feel like falling into an abyss. We often call this feeling craving. It is experienced as an empty aching, much like hunger or grief. Imagine yourself in a dark room. You are afraid of the dark. You call for help, but no one comes. Nothing you can do relieves the fear or takes away the dark. Your need to feel safe is just there, not being met. And it is the feeling that grows intolerable, not the dark. This is a taste of what that unbounded feeling is like. The body cannot tolerate the sensation of unboundedness for long. We are in constant need of stimuli and boundaries, without which we will go crazy, as sensory deprivation studies have shown (Murphy 1992). When infants cry, they are picked up and held by their caretakers. This is an example of a need being met—literally—by an act of the body being bounded by the arms of a loved one. There is a primal comfort in being held—our unbounded feeling is quite palpably bound, held safe and warm.

If the need is not going to be met, we must turn off the mechanism of longing, and we must still satisfy the craving with some substitute. We have to get rid of either the dark or our fear of it. Since we cannot make the darkness go away, we turn off the fear. Our bodies must first find some kind of relief. We will do what we can internally to accomplish this—hold our breath, depress sensation, take a rigid posture, or distract ourself with repetitive gestures. If none of this is enough, we will turn outside ourselves for more heavy-hitting relief.

Biological psychology studies have identified a condition called *learned helplessness* (Kalat 1988). In a study, researchers repeatedly exposed rats to electric shocks that they had no way of escaping. Subsequently, when they gave the animals shocks that they could easily escape, the animals made no effort to do so, even when goaded. They had learned to be helpless. If we are subjected to unrelenting, uncontrollable pain, we will habituate to it. If we consistently avoid enriching ourselves with rest, play, meditation, we will get used to that as well. Our bodies will not mobilize to take care of us. We can actually become addicted to not self-regulating, to not knowing what is good for us. To do this, we must turn off the internal body information that is basic to our sense of survival and happiness.

Addiction, according to the brain researchers R. A. Wise and M. A. Bozarth (Wise 1987), is also a condition of repeatedly moving toward something that is reinforcing. In this sense we can see addiction as the body's attempt to counteract learned helplessness by reaching for something. "If I can't have love, I'll take euphoria." "If I can't have safety, I'll take oblivion." We will move in ways that reach for whatever we can get. Addiction is in this sense a condition of boundary deficit. Our bodies simply keep reaching, reaching.

The Maturing Addiction

The addictive process, once it is etched in the body, can continue on its own momentum alone, fueled by continuing experiences of need deprivation or of reward for narrowly focusing. Thus our addiction matures as we mature. At some point in childhood, as development makes us more and more complex, body movement may not be enough to desensitize and keep increasingly complex pleasure and pain at bay. As the scope of our experience grows beyond physical survival, our feeling and our thinking can suffer from need deprivation, and we must increase the potency and dosage of pain relief and joy substitution in order to compensate. The complex behaviors of codependency are born, followed by rigidly held core beliefs (such as "there will never be enough," or "I am unlovable") and then ingestive practices like substance abuse. But the original movement behaviors remain, though they are usually modified to become more socially acceptable, mutating into slumps, shrugs, or nervous gestures such as head tilts, hair twirling, and finger tapping.

My own experience, coupled with reports from clients, leads me to believe that this developmental maturation of addiction follows the developmental stages of each person, much like a house follows its blueprint. At each stage the addiction has a characteristic structure: it goes in two directions, away from pain and toward pleasure. It follows the spiraling sequence and results described above, and it flows from the imprints from our earliest experiences of deprivation and from our genetic heritage, both of which are found in our physical body.

By uncovering and dealing with these patterns in each successive stage of addiction, and by providing appro-

priate interventions along the way, we can break through
to the root of addiction.

Love as a Boundary

Addiction is also a failure of the unconditional love that is
one of our greatest human needs. When we put conditions
on love, we decide to love only if, or only when a person
looks or behaves a certain way. It takes a lot of control
and effort to manage loving only parts of ourselves and
others. We constantly have to monitor their behavior to
decide if a person deserves our love or not. We develop
whole personalities in order to maximize the conditional
love. Sam Keen once wrote that "the greatest addiction of
all is to our personality—our routines, roles, and rigidi-
ties." Love is like air and water and sunlight. Without it
we will die. When we soak it up, we feel intense pleasure.
We grow. If love is made conditional upon how we act,
then we will develop an act to get it. It will seem like it
is the act that gets us the love we need. The act will feel
pleasurable, reinforcing. This is the second root of addiction, the need for the pleasure of love.

A few months ago a client who was three months into
her alcohol recovery came to her appointment reporting
that she had had a few drinks one day that week. As is
often the case, she told me that the week had been going
well, so well in fact that she and her boyfriend had gotten
very close. It was after this closeness happened that she
ended up drinking one day while he was away at work. As
she talked with me her body was both slumped and agitated, squirming around. I asked her how her body was
feeling right now, and she laughed and reported that she
hadn't been in her body since she woke up the morning of

her binge. When asked to turn her attention inward and go back home to her body, she felt anxious and reluctant. With some encouragement and patience, she began to report a tense clamping feeling in her throat. I asked her to allow this feeling to happen rather than attempt to relieve it. As she stayed with it, it progressed into a choking feeling. She suddenly remembered for the first time a childhood event when her abusive, alcoholic father had his hands around her neck, shaking her and yelling at her to be quiet after she had been running exuberantly through the house. She cried deeply at this point in the session, and came to realize that she had learned from this and other incidents not to get too happy, that being really joyful was dangerous. Drinking was one way to sedate her call to be really happy.

Addiction is two-directional: it is an attempt to anesthetize both the pain of unmet needs and the joy of need fulfillment, particularly the need for love. Love is both a need and a pleasure; its presence holds us in life's embrace. When we can receive it and generate it, we renew that embrace for ourselves and all those around us. The boundary that is created by that embrace is our body's true home, it is the suffusing glow of light and warmth radiating through the house of our body on a cold night.

3

The One-Two-Three Waltz
Body Patterns in Addiction

*I drink not from mere joy in wine nor to scoff at
faith—no, only to forget myself for a moment, that
only do I want of intoxication, that alone.*

—OMAR KHAYYAM

We leave our bodies by the use of off-handed movements,
breathing patterns, gestures, or postures that both mark
and alleviate an uncomfortable state. The movements also
soothe physically. When I urge clients to "go into" their
movement tags, allowing them to lead them where they
will, what is often uncovered is a feeling of lack, of not
being able to take care of oneself, of inherent wrongness,
of fear of death. This was vividly illustrated to me a few
years ago by a suicidal client whose movement tag would
begin with the dropping of her head toward her chest. She
would then begin to feel a strangling lack of air that pan-
icked her so much that she lifted her head, looked at me
very directly, and said, "I would rather die than feel that
feeling." Another client, who constantly battled food addictions, followed a seemingly simple gesture to her mouth
into terrified screams of, "I'm all alone! I'm all alone! No
one's there!"

I began to realize that the movements I was seeing had

their origin in early experiences. Time and again I saw a connection between early physical needs and the movements and behaviors I was studying. If an early need didn't get met adequately desensitization occurred and a behavioral gesture developed that was practiced whenever that deprivation was restimulated. The movement tag seemed to be a distorted self-comforting gesture, a kind of attempt to hold, stroke, or soothe.

And many times these deprivations were from preverbal times in the client's life, centering around such primal needs as warmth, nourishment, caring attention, and physical safety. The sequence of these movement habits also piqued my interest: a predictable flow of events emerged at the body level.

1. A feeling or memory or sensation starts to happen.
2. The movement gesture begins, and is repeated until the feeling stops or is relegated to just being talked about. The repeated movement is usually experienced as very compelling.
3. The person is very attached to what he or she is doing, finding the movement comforting or even pleasurable, and will become upset or resistant if anyone attempts to intervene to disrupt it.
4. The movement tag begins to diminish gradually. The person begins to "come down," feeling depressed, hopeless, or resentful. Frequent statements heard are, "Nothing every changes," "I'll never get out of this," or "I just can't do/get it."
5. Blame. "I am doing something wrong that I can't get through this," or "If you [therapist or friend] hadn't said that to me I would have felt a whole lot better." The basic result is self-hatred and shame.

It was discovering this sequence and its similarity to descriptions of the addictive process that first clued me in to the probability that I was seeing some kind of body-based addiction. This led me to a new operational definition of addiction: *Addiction is a person's consistent physical response, usually learned early in life, to a consistently unmet need.*

The response is intended to distract us from the pain of the unmet need, and to provide a substitute for the pleasurable experience of need satisfaction. Leaving our body gets us away from the pain or the threatening pleasure. Leaving our bodies soothes and comforts us at a time when we need it most.

As I have stated before, one of our basic needs is to experience and know that we are loved unconditionally. We don't have to be someone other than who we are to merit being loved. Who we are is inherently lovable. Ideally, an infant first experiences unconditional love from its parents, who are willing to attend to him or approve of who that child is. Unconditional love does not mean constant attention or praise; it means not withdrawing attention when things get sticky or uncomfortable, and not withdrawing basic positive regard. Many psychologists and writers, including Alice Miller, John Bradshaw, Gay and Kathlyn Hendricks, and others, have found that anyone with unhealed wounding (most of us) will withdraw attention and approval from anyone who stimulates their old pains. We snatch away our attention and approval in the face of the same kinds of experiences that caused it to be withdrawn from us. As children we will do almost anything to prevent our parents from practicing conditional love, including trying to be who our parents want us to be. This setup of fulfilling our parents' needs rather than being who we are is a basis of addiction. The need for love has more survival value than the need to be genuine. This sacrificing of genuineness in the service of getting love is very painful and crazy-making, but it keeps us alive.

Pain happens. Normally pain is experienced and then it is over, but when pain is not resolved, when it is experienced again and again with no solution, it is torture, senseless and unbearable, and the body will automatically take action to minimize it. What creates the need to use physical behaviors to sedate feeling experience? How do we recognize addiction in the body? Addictive behavior has five characteristics as I see it, and all five must be present for it to be considered addictive. They are:

1. Repetition
2. Lack of development
3. Lack of satisfaction
4. Lack of completion
5. Uncomfortable to watch

The first characteristic is repetition. The movement behavior is repeated, repeated, and repeated. This keeps the painful experience of feelings away, and provides a measure of soothing comfort. This behavior can be seen to resemble the rocking motions we see in children.

Second, the behavior lacks development—it doesn't change or go anywhere. It is always the same, feels the same, and has the same result. A nervous tug on one's chin does not develop into a pulling and then an angry pulling and then a genuine feeling of the original rage. It cycles around not going anywhere like a mouse in an exercise wheel.

Third, the behavior does not satisfy. It may feel comforting at the time, but the person will end up feeling vaguely odd, guilty, spaced out, or depressed.

Fourth, the action does not complete itself; it remains

unfinished in terms of the energy that drives it. It will look like a partial effort. A client I worked with habitually held her finger between her teeth whenever she was thinking. It looked like an incomplete biting action, and when she explored this tag she discovered that she did indeed want to bite.

Fifth, addictive actions are uncomfortable to watch. Observers will generally become either bored and withdrawn, judgmental, or frustrated and angry. I had a bulimic client a few years ago who would twirl a lock of her hair relentlessly during a session. There were times when I wanted to reach over and yank out that offending lock.

Often observing an addictive process in others will stimulate one's own addictive tendencies. If we can't get away from someone who is being addictive, we will feel an urge to practice our own addiction. In my case, when I wanted to yank out my client's hair I noticed that I would begin to rub my thumb against my index finger. These uncomfortable feelings are often misinterpreted as countertransference by therapists. In other words, therapists will see their frustration with clients as reflective of their own unresolved issues. This is true, but more importantly, as therapists we can begin to recognize what has stimulated our feelings, and get curious about potential addictions.

In the addictive process, we desensitize our body while inducing euphoria by means of a substance or a behavior. Desensitization and dissociation are important both to keep pain out of our awareness and to insulate us from feeling the toxic effects of the euphoria-producing substance or behavior. In order to continue to drink, for example, we have to ignore body messages that the alcohol makes us nauseous or light-headed or headachy. Desensitization and euphoria in tandem create the addictive process.

How do we use our body to withdraw from our body? Initially, we make repetitive gestures that hypnotize and anesthetize our physical experience. Try sitting in a chair and rocking back and forth for ten minutes, and notice how sedating this can be. Rocking chairs are meant to soothe in this way. This strategy of repetitive gestures is most frequently used by small children, but can be seen in psychotic and autistic people as well. As adults we resort to this primal strategy during times of stress by biting our nails, fluffing our hair, or tapping our feet.

Our next body strategy is to use tension as a desensitizer. Research has shown that tensing a muscle will, in the short run, increase sensation in that area. The nerves in the muscle get very active, both in maintaining the contraction and in giving the brain sensory feedback about the contraction. However, if the tension continues and becomes chronic, the nerves will tend to exhaust themselves and will only send sensory messages if there are large changes in the amount of tension. In other words, when tension becomes chronic, our nervous system begins to ignore it and pay attention to other things (the exception to this is when the tension actually causes damage to surrounding tissues, in which case the damaged tissues will complain loudly). Have you ever had a friend put his hand on your shoulder and exclaim how tight you are, only to be surprised because you weren't particularly aware of it?

We can only pay attention to one thing at a time. Another way we can desensitize ourselves out of our bodies is to practice paying attention to other things. As addicts we have two common ways of distracting ourselves from our here-and-now experience. The first is to pay attention only to our thoughts—to intellectualize. Anne Wilson-Schaef calls it "stinking thinking." We get very adept at rationalizing, excusing, fantasizing, conceptualizing, and analyzing. We can even run a good explanation of why we are the way we are. Even though our explanations can be technically accurate, they are used in the service of removing ourselves from our bodies, from directly experiencing the world.

Another favorite way of distracting ourselves is to pay exclusive attention to the environment around us. Getting focused on what is happening outside of us can be seen as the primary behavior of codependency. The addictions field has been the primary forum for the documentation and discussion of the phenomenon of codependency, seeing its origins in the dysfunctional family that can cause its members to be hypervigilant of others in order to feel safe and loved. While this focus of attention outside the self can indeed serve this function, we can also look at its function as a physical desensitizer. If we are constantly paying attention to the outside, we are ignoring our body.

We can use body processes to help distract our attention, whether they are internal, like runaway thinking, or external, like hypervigilance. Let's look now at very biological ways our bodies distract us. Hyperactivity and anxiety are physical phenomena partially created by adrenaline, a hormone produced in the adrenal glands, that prepares us either to fight or flee from danger. The more adrenaline we secrete, the more tendency we have to feel anxious and hypervigilant. The more we commit to these feelings, the more adrenaline we secrete. Our body, our emotions, and our thoughts all create a feedback loop that keeps us distracted from some more threatening awareness.

Depression is a kind of generalized, systematic desensitization. In depression, we use our mood and our level of physical activity to leave our bodies. It is the physical equivalent of turning down the volume on a stereo so that we can't hear the words to the music. In order not to hear the painful words stored in our bodies, we turn down all our physical functions, our feelings, and even our thoughts. It is a general anaesthetic, designed to get us away from a persistent physical message. Depression literally alters our body chemistry, slowing down the release of hormones, enzymes, and neurotransmitters (brain chemicals) that can help us feel energized and happy. This in turn can cause more depression, and the depression–body chemistry feedback loop keeps us stuck in a state of lessened aliveness.

We accomplish bodily desensitization in two other ways: with our breath and with our posture. It has long been noted by body-centered psychotherapists, among them Wilhelm Reich, Alexander Lowen, Stanley Keleman, and Gay Hendricks, that we can cut off feelings and sensations by cutting off our breath. The fuller we breathe, the more we feel; the less we breathe, the less we feel. By suppressing full breathing we can effectively fend off feeling. It has also been noted that posture can affect feeling and sensation. We have all noticed that when we are in good moods we sit straighter and walk taller, and that when in sad moods we tend to slump or collapse. This also goes in the other direction. Slumping can intensify or prolong a sad feeling. Thus, if we need the depressed feeling in order to avoid some other awareness, we can continue to slump or collapse as a way of helping this feeling stay in place.

Addictive behavior is repetitive, stays the same, is unsatisfying, remains incomplete, and is irritating to witness. All of these qualities must be present, and present in the body, for a behavior to be addictive. Many contemporary addictions theorists believe that addiction is more the rule than the exception in our society. If we add up the drug and alcohol addicts, the cigarette addicts, the food addicts, and the process addicts (those addicted to love, gambling, sex), we come up with an alarming percentage of the population. If we expand our definition of addiction to include anything we do that repeats, doesn't change, doesn't satisfy, doesn't complete, and irritates our loved ones, have we left anyone out?

Addiction in this sense is less a disease than a universal human condition. Buddhists would call addictive behavior our "habit energy," our natural tendency to be frightened of our awareness and aliveness. John Bradshaw says that addiction always has life-damaging consequences. Yet this same process, practiced to a lesser extent, can be said to have life-limiting qualities. It is possible that the difference between life-damaging and life-limiting is found in a genetic or chemical imbalance in the brains of certain people. We must continue to investigate the real possibility that heavy-duty substance abuse has independent biological mechanisms that result in a propensity to self-destruct. Life-limiting behaviors also deserve our full attention. Here we are not looking so much at healing woundedness as we are at freeing ourselves to grow, transform, and become more expanded and happy as human beings.

All addictions, whether to cocaine or shopping or negative thinking, share the same features mentioned above. We can speculate that there are some shared processes in all of them and that we are also looking at a continuum of dysfunction. Recovery can also be on this line. Figure 2

shows the continuum of progress from addiction to recovery to transformational growth.

We threaten our lives when we introduce large amounts of toxins into our bodies. We damage our lives when we practice addictions that cause long-term illness or break the fabric of our families and societies. We limit our lives when we fail to grow, when we keep ourselves sedated or distracted, when we fail to contribute to others. We promote life when we commit to our own happiness and the happiness of others. Moving from life-threatening to life-promoting actions is a tremendous step. Some of us have been less traumatized by life and have less distance to travel than others. Whatever the distance, reclaiming and reoccupying our bodies is the way toward affirming happiness, toward reconnecting with the exquisite beauty of life.

Replacing Boundaries with Defenses

When we don't have adequate boundaries, when the needing goes on and owing to our ignorance or powerlessness, we erect defensive structures so that we will not fall apart in the slightest breeze. Defenses are a second set of boundaries that we set in place when our natural boundaries are not functioning or are not adequate. Defenses keep threatening things out, or in. They are a suit of armor that signals, "I expect the worst," so that when someone or something meets up with us, instead of having contact we typically have a skirmish. We all have to be able to defend ourselves against real danger, and we have inherited this ability from our ancestors genetically, in a process that reaches all the way back to single-celled life. It is interesting to look at the archetypal defense strategies that have worked for our ancestors, because they have passed them on to us. As complex animals, the three basic options we have when we fell threatened are: fight, flee, or freeze. Below is a list of defense strategies characteristic of various animals that can stand as symbols for the different types of human defense strategies.

Fight

Badger. Using all-out attack as a defense. Attacking with such rage and determination that, no matter what size you are, you are totally intimidating. This type of person concentrates strength in his/her jaws and arms and has movement patterns of bursting forward. This strategy would describe a person who tends to sit quietly, and then (seemingly) all of a sudden explodes into a frightening rage.

Bear. Using size, strength, and a sound to intimidate. Getting bigger to display one's power. Being over"bear"-ing or insensitive. Strength in this person is more evenly distributed throughout the body, though the arms are used extensively. Usually this person is considered slower and less cunning, but this is not necessarily true. This kind of person is someone who typically gets into funks or bad moods, and whose family learns to avoid them during these times.

Flight

Gazelle. Using speed and agility to outrun and outmaneuver a predator. The body of this kind of person is characterized by hyperalertness, large eyes, and the ability to burst away from perceived danger at an angle. The classic example of this defense is the "I'm outta here!" maneuver: "When things get rough, I gotta get going." This person perceives the world to be frightening and overwhelming. He or she may not be able to stay with an intense interaction.

Prairie Dog. Using speed, but primarily broken running, or dodging, to reach safety. The body of this kind of person is usually characterized by crouching, a low center of gravity, and powerful legs. This strategy is hard to pin down. Just when you think you are having a meaningful dialogue with this person, you look around and wonder where they've gone. This strategy uses distraction and hiding out as tactics.

Freezing

Rabbit. Holding completely still so that you will not be noticed. Hiding through stillness. A person with this kind of body is able to hold still all over, even for long periods of time. This defense plan is often used by children, as it is by small animals with no other means of defense. It operates on the assumption that freezing up will make a threat go away.

Chameleon. Hiding out by blending in with the environment. Becoming invisible. This person's body can be very adaptive—it will take on the characteristics of whomever or whatever is around, sometimes using ruse and deception was well as hiding. This person will appear to agree with you in order that conflict will be minimized.

Opossum. Playing dead—literally turning down life functions so that a predator will lose interest. The body of this person can become pale, and breathing very shallow. This behavior is typical of a suicidal person, someone who feels so threatened by life that they would rather die. This strategy is typically used only in extreme life-or-death situations, or when an emotion or thought feels life threatening. I had a client who employed this strategy who would sit for hours on the couch, then wake up abruptly, realizing he did not remember anything about the previous hours. He had been severely beaten as a child, and was suicidal.

Turtle. Creating a shell and contracting into it to form an impenetrable barrier, while remaining visible. The body goes still and expressiveness diminishes. Frequently interpreted as stubbornness.

As humans, our bodies are familiar with all these techniques, and will adopt them under stress. The freezing options are more useful when we are threatened as small children. Fight is adopted more often when we are big and have been exposed to violence or extensive rough play. Notice your own body strategies under stress, and see if any of these animals best describe your defensive strategies. Does any one or combination of these patterns feel familiar? Do any of them describe certain family members?

We can usually recognize defensiveness in other people and we can often feel ourselves adopting our own responding defenses too. We can eliminate much of our need for defense, though, by learning to generate our own boundaries. Boundaries are physical, emotional, and cognitive. They represent the simple statement "This is my limit." They are about defining ourselves and taking care of ourselves. They identify us to ourselves and others. And they are created through consistent need fulfillment.

Let's look at a primal need like hunger. It begins with our stomach rumbling and tightening. These need-signals from the body set us on a possible course of action. We become aware that we are hungry, and this awareness is a self-defining act—"I am hungry; it is me that is hungry." Eating is another self-affirming act—"I am full; I am no longer hungry." We have responded to our need and we have met it, and this meeting the need forms a boundary, one that is permeable to every-changing circumstances. What would happen if we didn't eat? The hunger would continue, would get louder and more insistent. The need would not be met by a self-affirming act; in fact, not eating would become a self-negating act. If we continue to negate ourselves, we loose energy, and eventually we will loose the hunger signals. Our body will get the message that it cannot self-regulate, and a distorted or inadequate perception of who (and where) we really are results.

Defenses come in as a secondary attempt to create a boundary when need fulfillment fails. If we cannot self-regulate and self-define, we create a defensive boundary out of anticipation, projection, anxiety, and fear. Defenses are like body reflexes—they may be quick, but they're kind of stupid. They can be triggered by any stimulus, much as your knee will jerk when struck, whether in serious danger of injury or by the doctor checking your reflexes. I can't begin to count the times I've been embarrassed to realize that I was assuming someone was being hostile when it was only such a defensive reaction.

When we get in the habit of not meeting our needs, we accept a cumbersome substitute: defensiveness. Defensiveness has a twin sister; her name is denial. Just as our knee

jerks before we are even aware of it, defensiveness is a sign
of the negation of experience that hallmarks denial. If I am
defending myself, if I am in fight/flee/freeze mode, I will
deny any reality that does not conform with the skirmish I
think I am defending myself against. If I feel like prey, I
must deny any perception of you as anything other than a
predator. This is how denial adheres to addiction.

In Buddhism there exists a wisdom which states that it
is our nature to try to grasp on to and keep things we like
and to push away and negate things we don't like. These
things can be objects, emotions, thoughts, anything from
a new car to a scary feeling. We all want to hold on to the
good feeling and get rid of the bad feeling. Most all my
clients come into therapy with the express purpose of getting rid of meddlesome emotions and behaviors, while en-
abling themselves to feel the good stuff. On one hand, this
makes sense. Who wouldn't want to have a good life?
What Buddhism states, however, is that the way we go
about pursuing this good life is the key to making it happen or not.

First of all, we have to go back to the statement that
pain happens. It is highly doubtful that we could get
through our lives without the pain of our dog dying, without falling down and hurting ourselves, or without some
other injustice, illness, or discomfort. I have one client who
has two sons who are both dying of separate illnesses.
How can all these things only happen to other people and
not us?

And as far as the good stuff goes, there also looms the
concept of impermanence. Whatever is, passes. Orgasms
don't keep going and going. When scientists have repeti-
tively stimulated the pleasure centers of rats' brains, it was
found that for a time they appeared to be having a grand

orgiastic time, but that soon they became passive and dull, still reaching for the pleasure button, but neglecting each other and food and everything else. In other words, they became profound addicts. Pleasure passes, but the good news is that impermanence applies to pain too. Pain also passes. Both are impermanent. The art of life then lies in going with this flow rather than trying to control it. Happiness arises not out of pushing away pain and pushing the pleasure button. That makes us into addicts, and causes untold suffering. Happiness comes when we dance with the flow, when we participate with whatever arises. So we come upon the radical idea that happiness is not about how many good times we've had and bummers we haven't had, but from being willing to greet life as it occurs, to meet it and respond in its gush and flow. We don't attach ourselves to the contents of life, but we celebrate the very process of being alive.

I have heard that for us North Americans, baseball is a metaphor for life. This is aptly illustrated in *The Brothers K,* a marvelous novel by James Duncan. Near the end of the book there is a funeral for a pro baseball player. During the family gathering after the funeral, his daughter is talking about something her father once said to her:

> He said there are two ways for a hitter to get the pitch he wants. The simplest way is not to want any pitch in particular. But the best way, he said—which sounds almost the same, but is really very different—is to want the very pitch you're going to get. Including the one you can handle. But also the one that's going to strike you out looking. And even the one that's maybe gonna bounce off your head (Duncan 1992, 690).

Our suffering occurs not so much when pain happens as when we try to control our experience of life. By trying to

pick and choose what experiences we should have and
which ones we shouldn't have, we practice our first addiction—control. Expending effort to control our experience
forces us to deny parts of ourselves and others. This denial
requires desensitization, and on into the Addictive Spiral
we go. Grasping onto or pushing away experience then
involves one of the defensive strategies listed above. This
does not mean that we need to remain passive to life. All
that life requires is that we dance with it, being an active
partner. We get ourselves on the Addictive Spiral if we
deny our pleasure as well as our pain. Passing up an ice
cream cone can be just as addictive as indulging in it.

Dance is a splendid metaphor here. We are born on to a
dance floor called experience. Life is our partner. If we try
to take control and lead, life will step on our toes. If we
remain still and limp, life will give up and go find a new
partner. Either way, we suffer greatly in the absence of the
greatest relationship we can ever know.

Last week, I stubbed my toe on a chair leg. My son
watched as I hopped around, cursed, and attempted to
hold my toe and move at the same time. When my theat-
rics calmed down, he pointed out that I looked goofy in
the extreme, and he proceeded to imitate my awkward
antics. Within moments my toe was forgotten as we
laughed and played a holding-your-toe-and-hopping
game.

Earlier this year, a friend of mine, a young man of six-
teen named Matt, died of leukemia. I was devastated that
such a joyous spirit should be gone so soon, and I was
feeling a profound sorrow. I remember coming home from
his funeral, sitting on the sofa and looking out the window
at an apple tree outside. I cried for a while and looked at
the tree. I began to notice the intense green of the leaves,

the way the branches bent and snapped as the squirrels scampered through them. All of a sudden, I saw a light imbedded in the tree, a kind of luminous aliveness permeating it. I felt I was able to directly see the tree in a way I never had before—sap pulsing, leaves shimmering. I have now named that tree Matt's tree, and consider it his monument.

So it is a move of sometimes choosing to have an ice cream, and sometimes not. Which choice will affirm our aliveness, will keep us dancing with our awesome partner, life? Similarly, we don't have to choose hair shirts in order to keep in step. When pain occurs we dance with it by asking ourselves, What is life requiring of me right now? We can fall in love with the very coming and goings of experience. We are ourselves, dancing. We define ourselves not by the contents of the movie on the screen (in which case we will get caught in various flee/fight/freeze scenarios), but with the light beam that makes the movie possible. It is here where we join the elite corps of truly happy people.

Finding the Physical Boundaries Again

Reclaiming the choosing of life is what we are recovering. We are not recovering *from* something so much as recovering *into* something. My thesaurus gives as its first synonym for *recover* "to find again." How do we find again our ability to choose life? How do we actively meet our needs so that we form the boundaries that allow us to consciously choose life? When our needs do not get met as children, it is not so much those needs that we ultimately lose, for we can arrange to provide them, but our ability to know how actively to meet any need. We habituate to the act of not meeting needs. We forget how to dance. To restore our dancing skills, we can look to our bodies.

Let's think of ourselves as a single-celled organism. We are made up of a cell wall (a boundary), with lots of good goop inside. Our life functions require that we take in nourishment and excrete waste in order to keep the organism going. This requires a relationship with the outer environment, which is where the nourishment and waste treatment facilities lie. So our boundary has a dual function: it must encircle and define us, keeping that which is not us out; and it must let in that which will fuel and sustain us. To keep things out, the boundary must be strong. To let things in, it must be willing to open up.

We can say that there are three possible states for us to be with regard to boundaries, whether we are single-celled or billion-celled. These three states are: fusion, contact, and isolation (as illustrated in figure 3). Fusion is a process of merging. It happens when boundaries diffuse, and it results in a free mixing of material. A good example of this is conception, when sperm penetrates egg and the mixing of parental DNA begins. In isolation, boundaries become so strong that materials can neither get in nor out. This resembles what we attempt to do when we try to encase spent nuclear fuel. In between fusion and isolation is con-

fusion   contact   isolation

FIG. 3.

tact, a state where boundaries are in place yet permeable. The cell is capable of choosing what to let in and out as each unique event requires. All the cells in our body have permeable membranes to a greater or lesser degree. There are times when it is of benefit for a cell to isolate. In this way it can keep out poisons or prevent its own destruction. In rare instances the merging action of fusion is called for—without it there would be no conception of new life. But where cells like to be most is in the permeable state of contact, where they can dance with impermanence, responding appropriately to the spontaneous moves of life.

If we understand the single cell as a microcosm of our multi-billion–celled bodies, the same principles apply. At times, life asks us to melt a bit, to merge. I recall the feeling of merging that characterized the period when I was nursing my infant son. In this case, the merging was called bonding, and it was what enabled me to weather the 3:00 A.M. feedings, the colic, and all the poop. There are also times when it can be appropriate to isolate, for example, I will not be around cigarette smoke, and I do not stand near X-ray machines or people who are in a rage.

When I choose fusion as a consistent strategy, I choose defense rather than boundary, and I fall into the classic addiction of codependency, the tendency to lose myself in others. When I choose isolation as a strategy, I also adopt defense, and cut myself off from any nourishment the world could provide. Like the over-pleasured rats, I will feed off my own body until I die. When I don't pay adequate attention to what life is asking of me, I am incapable of choosing it, of meeting myself through meeting my needs. I rely instead on fusion, letting others take care of me, or isolation, where I renounce others and try to be separate. Either strategy will kill me eventually, if practiced consistently enough. If I practice these in any kind of habitual way, I actually *become* a poison to myself and others; I become a drain on the society which must either carry me or dispose of me.

My body is the place where I learn and relearn the difference between choosing and grasping and pushing away. I can feel when I am permeable, fused, or isolated. When I am permeable, my body feels alert and relaxed at the same time. I am breathing fully, and my body moves happily and economically. When I fuse, I can't locate my body, I don't have much sensation, and I feel the presence of fight/ flee/freeze somewhere in my musculature and physiology. When I isolate, I also feel my defenses. In fact, that is all I feel. My awareness is dominated by my defense sensations, whether they are depressing my physiological processes or hyperactivating them. In either case, I can't read the environment accurately. It either looks like me, or like a suspicious alien.

But it is in contact where I have the most fun. I am still myself, but I am also the delicious cookie I am eating; I am as luminous as the tree before me. By being permeable, I don't become the tree or the cookie, but for a moment, I do become delicious and luminous, because I am having that experience. And I can only do this by actively choosing life. I bring in the cookie and the tree as dance partners, momentary representatives of life.

The state of being permeable is where most of our joy resides, where our pleasure and others' pleasure in us dwells. Our joy derives not so much from the ice cream, but from the willingness to be permeable to the experience of it. Our satisfaction in life comes not from pushing away the grief, but in feeling so moved and filled and permeated by it that we come to the center of all life. I now really know how alive my friend Matt was, and feel the immense privilege of having witnessed his presence here. And I have the apple tree to remind me.

Finding the Cognitive Boundaries Again

Our minds engage in this same boundary/defense process, and need their own special form of attention in order to stay permeable. Our minds have specialized functions, such as the abilities to remember and to plan. These two abilities that are not consistently present in other animals are crucial to our self-identity as individuals and as a species. Both are of great benefit, but they also have costs—they take us out of the present moment, out of our direct experience: as I plan my week next week, I am not aware of the mosquito on my arm, and I get bitten. Planning lets us dissociate in service of a higher purpose. Ideally, we oscillate our attention in and out of direct experience on a consistent basis so that we can benefit from both functions. But if we go for too long in plan-assess-remember mode, we will feel fatigued and will need some sort of rest or recreation (something direct and experiential, like play) to reestablish our equilibrium. How many of us set ourselves up to overdo in this manner! If we spent the whole day in direct experience we would be like infants, our attention going toward whatever happens to be in front of our faces at the moment. That kind of behavior doesn't get dinner cooked, and it is why infants need constant care and attention.

So, we need both states. If we indulge in one or the other for too long, we will have some major paying back to do. Optimal benefit derives from oscillating back and forth between the two states. How do we optimalize this oscillation cognitively? We have already seen that coming into our senses, focusing our attention on the here and now gives us direct experience. There is also a way to go into the mind and focus our attention so that we spend our mental energy in a satisfying way. In direct experience we sense the world clearly. The equivalent process in the mind is perception.

Edmund Jacobson (1967) called perception designated sensation. In other words, perception is sensation that has been processed by the mind. Sensory signals travel up our spinal cord and enter our brain, where they are compared with our memory to see if we have had an experience like this before. It is our nature to categorize incoming sensation into grids of meaning so that the world is not chaotic. This way, each time we pick up a potato we don't have to go about an extensive exploratory process in order to understand it. We simply compare the thing in our hand to our existing category *potato,* and a fit occurs. Potato!

My grid of meaning labeled *potato* has other things in it, things that I associate with it. In my grid is also *delicious, grows underground, french fries,* and *potato famine* (I'm part Irish). In another person's grid might be *yuck, gives me gas, lumpy mess at Thanksgiving I was forced to eat,* and so forth. Clearly, we order our worlds differently.

Our families, cultures, religions, and personal histories guide us in constructing our grids of meaning. If I have been raised with a father in the Ku Klux Klan, I will have *nigger* and *low-life* in the same grid with African-American. Grids of meaning give order to our world; they also define and shape it. They set us up for particular behaviors. Our grids seem to represent reality, but they are merely pigeonholes for sorting and storing data. Depending on the sorting, the world can look like either a hostile battleground or a sylvan glade. We can actually become a slave to these categories, refusing to pay attention to information that contradicts or upsets their status quo. And this attentional denial, as we have seen before, is the hallmark of addiction. The existing grids of meaning become more important than having a direct relationship to ourselves and the world.

How then do we work to create grids that maximize our happiness and the happiness of others? When we attend to the process of gridding, taking conscious care of how we form our categories, we build cognitive structures that serve rather than run us. Meditation is an ancient discipline that focuses our attention in this way. My meditation and spiritual teacher, Thich Nhat Hanh, once told me, "All views are wrong views, but since it is in our nature to have views, we should relax, and attend to keeping them as accurate as possible." He then gave us the Are-You-Sure? practice. In this practice, we contemplate our views about ourselves and the world, and then ask ourselves the question, "Am I sure?" I instituted this practice with a paranoid client last year. Through using it in connection with casual contacts he had with people on the street, he was able to see that he wasn't really sure that people were suspicious of him at all. He began to observe his paranoid thinking, oscillating his attention inside as well as out to others, and to see his thoughts as separate from what the people around him were doing.

I will write in later chapters about other techniques for taking good care of our grids of meaning, keeping them permeable to new ideas and information and to feedback from others. The oscillation of attention is particularly good at bathing our views with fresh water. It permits us to nourish our grids constantly with raw data from direct experience so that the grids have a chance to adapt and flourish. It helps us to avoid too much isolation, which will rigidify our views, and too much fusion, which will merge our views with whatever others that happen along. In this way, our categories can be in direct contact with the world, opening us up to a mutually nourishing relationship with it.

What does the process of gridding look like? Figure 4 illustrates it. It begins with an event, a stimulus. This stimulus impacts on our senses, and in the act of perceiving it, we describe it. Let's say my friend comes over to my house, and as she comes through the door, she smiles at me and my son. The description phase would involve labels such as *corners-of-mouth-turning-up*, and *squeezing-around-eyes*. Both my son and I could report observing this and for both of us, the perceptual box is categorized as *smile*. Let's say further that my smile box has in it a memory of my childhood girlfriend always smiling at me right before she was about to say something mean. And my son hasn't had this experience. So he will have in his smile box memories of smiling being associated with approval and fun. Now that we are both referenting to our smile boxes, our

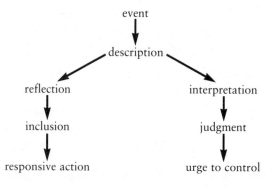

FIG. 4.

experiences can begin to differ. We will each interpret, vis-à-vis our own history. I will assume that my friend is about to criticize me, and my son will assume that he is in for a good time.

As soon as we interpret, we mix our direct experience and our description of it with our history, and we assume this experience is going to be like the past ones it outwardly resembles. But there is another possibility. We can oscillate our attention and get more raw data. In the above case, by really taking in my friend, really seeing that she is herself, not my childhood girlfriend. This will help me to keep my grids clean and relevant to the present moment. This action is called reflection. My son also can reflect and keep himself from forming an expectation that he will be attended to and played with. We can get back to reflection even if we have started to interpret by using the Are-You-Sure? practice.

If I have stayed with interpretation, I will then move to judgment. It is a quick step from the smile to the assumption of criticism, to anger in advance that I am going to be treated this way. Judgment involves making a value statement—something is good or bad. In this case, I make my friend bad. My son, if he stays with interpretation, will make her good. If something is good, we want to go toward it, and if something is bad we want to push it away. We will either grasp or reject. Our friend is no longer our friend but an object of our desires.

If I have oscillated attention and stayed in reflection, the next step is inclusion. I include my friend in with my awareness of that memory being stimulated. I allow these two events to be with me and to be unique at the same time. My son includes our friend in with his memories of fun and approval, and can see them as distinct.

If judgement has won out, my last step is the urge to control. If it seems that my friend is going to criticize me momentarily, I will shore up my defenses in anticipation. I will need to control both her and my experience in order to push away the bad that I don't want to feel. Maybe I will choose the badger defense. I might say to her, "Well, what do you want? What are you doing here?" My son might say, "You're going to play with me, aren't you?" In either case, my friend hasn't been greeted, she's been assaulted with control.

Out of inclusion, we can have responsive action. I invite my friend in. And when we begin to visit and she asks me how I'm doing, I can tell her how I just had this memory, stimulated by her smile, of being hurt by my childhood friend. I then have an opportunity to talk and feel it out, healing myself and bonding with my friend all at once. The actions I take reflect the accuracy of my experience, and those kinds of actions are always nourishing for all involved. My son might ask for us to play with him, but without the compulsion to *make* us play with him. In such an atmosphere of nourishment, play can be a great idea.

Our bodies and minds will defend themselves when they are habituated to not self-regulating, not actively meeting nourishment needs. When we meet, touch, make contact with ourselves directly, this very act fulfills needs and creates boundaries. These boundaries can also breathe, they can remain permeable to the pulse and beat of life. Life becomes real and fresh, not an automatic reenactment of the way we have always had it done to us. When we have habituated to an unsatisfying, scripted life, we need specific strategies to unravel the plot and begin a new, more fulfilling story.

4

Recovering Our Body
The Moving Cycle

Why not wake up this morning?
—RUMI

The traditional addictions-recovery programs pioneered by people such as Claudia Black, John Bradshaw, Charles Whitfield, and Sharon Wegscheider-Cruse all incorporate the twelve-step program that originated with AA. Requirements of this program, such as scrupulous honesty and taking responsibility for one's actions, are essential to any form of addiction treatment and to any means of reclaiming aliveness. I have developed a four-stage process that I call the Moving Cycle, that takes aspects of existing recovery strategies, includes them, and adds to them. The Moving Cycle introduces experiences designed to transform addictive behavior from an unconscious, insufficient need substitute into a conscious and satisfying action. When we move through this cycle, we not only wake up in the morning, we can also wake up in all the rest of our lives.

The Moving Cycle is a process-oriented model. It does not assume specific goals or outcomes. Each traveler on the cycle determines his or her own goals and interests in it. This at the outset counters one of the original wounds of addiction—that family agendas and rules imposed on us may have forced us to take on a different form than who we really are. The Moving Cycle was developed out of years of watching the natural healing and transformation process. When left to themselves, healing and growth seem to follow distinct movement sequences. There are four stages, and successful completion of one promotes the next. The fourth stage promotes the first to occur again at a deeper and more profound level.

The Moving Cycle operates on the same principle as Chinese handcuffs. Remember that woven bamboo tube you put on your two index fingers? If you pulled away to get your fingers out, the bamboo squeezed and your fingers became more trapped. You had to gently move your fingers farther into the tube to get free. In an analogous way, the Moving Cycle assumes that the only way out of addiction is through it: through the feelings, through the sensations, through the old limits, further into the body that is our home. The Moving Cycle can be an experience of coming home.

The first stage of the cycle is *Awareness*. We have seen that one of the primary features of addiction is the tendency to desensitize. To undo this often ancient pattern,

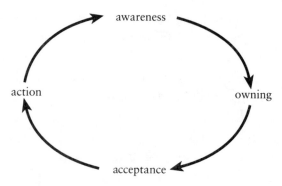

FIG. 5. THE MOVING CYCLE

awakeness and sensation must be returned to the body. This is both a frightening and an enlivening process. When we first begin to resensitize, we often reexperience old pains. Having the courage to do just this—to acknowledge the feeling instead of cutting it off—is crucial. It is similar to the first step in the twelve-step program, where we admit we are addicted. In the first stage of the Moving Cycle, we acknowledge what we feel, or what we weren't letting ourselves feel. This starts out as a very physical process, one of tracking and reporting sensations in the body in order to reawaken our natural ability to tell when we are harming ourselves. The ability to assess harm is what we have to ignore in order to cut off hated parts of ourselves and to practice addiction. By acknowledging what is going on in our bodies, we also rekindle our ability to sense pleasure. Reclaiming our ability to reward ourselves is also crucial in the process. Awareness forms the primary building block of direct experience, which is what we are trying to recover.

How do we cultivate what Fritz Perls calls "organismic self-regulation"? We begin with sensory awareness. Our ability to feel and express our physical experience is the foundation of recovery, the bedrock of joyful and satisfying action in the world. Statements such as "My head is pounding" or "My feet feel heavy" are acts of repatriation, empowerment, and reoccupation of our most tangible self. They are literally the fuel for the transformative journey.

The second stage I call *Owning*. This is the act of telling the complete truth about one's experience, of seeing everything that occurs within us to be our own creation. We all tend to distance ourselves from our experience by denying it or projecting it out onto others. This creates blame, excuses, and rationalizations that serve to rob us of our power to resolve hurts. Addicts are famous for being the most highly adept liars and sneaks in the world, mostly because these strategies are essential for keeping the addictive process going. Anne Wilson-Schaef goes so far as to define addiction as anything we need to lie about. Telling the truth is an act of taking responsibility for our experience. In other words, we are 100 percent responsible for what we are feeling and doing right now. When we take 100 percent of the responsibility for our current experience, not confusing it with childhood woundings (for which we were not responsible), we can then reclaim the power to do things differently. As long as we make others responsible for how we feel or for what is happening to us, we give them power over our very aliveness, and the only way we can feel alive is to control them. Taking responsibility cuts through codependency as well. Telling the truth is necessary to touch the original pain of unmet needs and to restore self-regulation.

Taking responsibility for our experience is the equivalent of the fourth, fifth, eighth, ninth, and tenth steps in AA recovery—making a moral inventory of ourselves, admitting our wrongs, and working to make amends for them. In the body this process is connected to the ability to not only *have* a feeling but to *sustain* it, to let it move us. By staying curious to a sensation rather than squashing it, we access our ability to let it inform and change us. We access our most basic and creative response—in which our body moves through a feeling freely without any conditions or limitations. This reawakening of our creativity comes from taking responsibility for our experience, from acknowledging the essential statement, "This is me feeling this, doing this."

How do we work with the Owning stage in the body? The essential problem behind the inability to take responsibility is a lack of boundaries, or inadequate limits. A need creates an energetic rush in the body, as we have seen. This rush of energy, in order to be resolved, must be met with a container or a boundary. When an infant is picked up and held, a boundary of love, warmth, and protection is created. This action by the caregiver is a primal response that lets the infant know that there is someone out there responding to its need to be held in safety. When needs are not met with such a boundary, the body's energy continues to rush out into space. This kind of unbounded energy is frightening on a primal level—the feeling is similar to falling off a cliff through open space. When my clients begin to reexperience this state of unbounded energy they most often report feeling that they are going to die. It is this unbounded feeling in the body that people practice addiction to avoid. The addictive movement, behavior, belief, or substance provides some kind of sensory boundary.

In movement therapy, the Owning phase is one of sensing the natural internal limits of our body and its processes and containing our energy within it. It involves allowing a sensation to evolve into an emotion and allowing that emotion to be felt fully. To do this, we must practice letting our bodies be containers for feelings. We relearn to trust our bodies in this phase. We experience that we can feel feelings all the way, and not only do we not die when we do, but we feel more alive. Our boundary is actually felt, and we can feel safe and secure that our feelings occur within us and that others' feelings occur outside of us. To address codependency issues, we must be able to sense the difference between our own and other people's movement energy, and still keep our own boundaries. Often in this stage clients will work with creating physical boundaries, limits, and structures.

The third stage is *Acceptance*. This is the stage in which we address our core imprints of shame and wrongness. Shame lives in the body in several ways. First, it translates into a poor body image, affecting our ability to sense accurately our body or its processes. We criticize its size, shape, or performance. We see it as something we have to drag along, something that weighs us down. Second, an imprint of wrongness always lodges in certain parts of the body, causing tension, desensitization, injury, or illness. Sexual shame will tend to lodge in the pelvis. A feeling of powerlessness will often pull the chest down and back. We can experience headaches, throat tension, and stomach pains, all as an acting out of specific imprints of shame. But third, and most important of all, the lack of love that we feel for ourselves affects our breathing. By constricting our breathing we cut off our ability to feel, thereby defending ourselves from unrequited pain or threatening pleasure.

Full breathing creates space in our bodies for new sensations to emerge and literally provides the oxygen that we need to become more alive. It also establishes a container for feelings to be held and formed in. Breathing into a feeling helps us take responsibility for it as an experience that we ourselves are generating, not one that other people are pushing onto us. It creates both the boundaries needed in order to form and feel the feeling as well as the space to express and finish it fully. It results in a reprogramming of love where before there was only lack.

Acceptance in the body involves breathing into whatever feelings emerge, allowing our bodies to completely move what they feel, and practicing a nonjudgmental, loving attitude towards the emerging dance. No experience is better than another; it is simply the current situation, and it warrants our unconditional attention. The Latin word for breath is the origin of the word *spirit*. The Acceptance phase is a reclaiming of our spirituality—our sense that God is love, and that our job is to be love, in love, of love, for love. The concept of recovery involving spirituality permeates the twelve steps of AA, and reembodying love starts with loving our bodies.

The Acceptance phase has to do with getting the love back. Addiction has in its roots a failure of love, and we must not only process our woundedness about this failure, but we must also teach ourselves to love again. We first recover loving ourselves, then we re-learn to love others. The most essential component of learning to love is the ability to make a commitment, which is similar to the concept of surrender found in AA. In making our commitment to love more important than anything that can interfere with it, we surrender our allegiance to the stances, positions, beliefs, and behaviors that drain love from our lives—in other words, we learn to make love unconditional.

In the Awareness phase, our job is to awaken to direct experience through the senses. The Owning phase is about sustaining this awakened state through any feelings that occur. Acceptance, then, occurs when we have ridden the feeling through to completion, and we are willing to let go of it. It has completely moved through us and changed us, and now we relax the body to release it. Emptying our bodies of these feelings allows love to surge in.

The last phase in recovery is the *Action* phase. The Action phase begins when we can sustain uncritical and loving attention to ourselves. With this ability we can move out into the world in a healthy manner, one in which our presence becomes a force for positive change in everything around us. The Action phase involves relating to the world in the same awake, responsible, accepting way that we relate to ourselves. In the body, it involves movement that is communicative. In a therapy session, it may take the form of the client speaking while breathing deeply, or putting the newly discovered sensations and expressions into action by walking, talking, or relating to others. It is making sure that the change that has occurred in the session will be embodied in our daily life and relationships. It reflects the twelfth step of the twelve-step programs—the step in which we practice our awakening and carry our message to others. In the Action phase of the Moving Cycle, we carry our bodies out onto the dance floor of life.

The assumption inherent in the Action phase is that in order for change to become real, in order for love to mean anything, it must be manifested in the world. For new awareness to occur, for a new Moving Cycle to begin, we must exercise our previous changes outside ourselves. Action makes us producers in the world rather than just consumers, to use Gay Hendricks's expression.

The four phases of the Moving Cycle combine to form a sequence that promotes recovery and transformation on all levels: physical, emotional, cognitive, and spiritual. The phases occur both within a single experience and throughout the length of recovery. Within a single experience the cycle can start out with talking about an issue while noticing what comes up in the body and describing the sensation and quality of the experience. We can then focus on the experience, allowing it to deepen and develop within the boundaries of continuing to tell the truth about it. As the experience carries us through the uncharted waters of thoughts, feelings, and sensations expressed to their completion, we may find the inherent need satisfaction in self-regulation and can feel friendly to every nook and cranny of our being. We can then apply this new sequence to our outer world, practicing using the sequence in relation to others.

A Moving Cycle in a therapeutic setting can look much like the session I will now describe. This session took place at the Addictions Recovery Center in Boulder, Colorado, where I worked for several years. My client was a recovering alcoholic, three months into her sobriety. We had been working together for a month, and in this time I had gotten to know her history, had taught her how to breathe deeply, and had familiarized her with being aware of sensation in her body.

She came in agitated, talking a mile a minute. She reported that her boss had threatened to fire her if she showed up late for work one more time. She launched into a litany of complaint that basically carried the theme of her boss as a Nazi jerk who didn't understand all the different stresses she had in her life, and who cares exactly when she shows up, the work is stupid anyway, and furthermore he's not such an angel anyway because he lies to his employees all the time, and so forth. The tirade showed all the signs that it would go on for quite some time, with further elaborations of the woe-is-me theme. I noticed that I began to feel slightly irritated, wondering when she was going to stop.

I also noticed that as she vented her anger she was alternately raising and lowering her shoulders in a shrugging motion of which she seemed unaware. When she paused for a moment, I asked her to check in with herself and with how she was feeling right now. At first she was reluctant to do this. She complained to me that I never wanted to

listen to her and only wanted to hear about her stupid
body. I assured her that this accusation was in many ways
true—I did not want to hear her stories but wanted to listen deeply to her essential self, which seemed to be getting
lost behind her words. She paused, and her eyes got wide
and began to fill with tears. She closed her eyes and reported that her heart was beating fast, that she felt angry
and ashamed, and that she felt like crying. I observed that
her shoulders were slightly hunched, and that they had
been alternately going up and down while she had been
talking.

I asked her to pause for a while and just pay attention
to how she was feeling, especially in her shoulders. She
closed her eyes again and turned her attention inside, noting that she felt tense all across her upper back. I then
asked her to intensify this tension and see what happened.
When she did so, her shoulders raised and squinched inward. I encouraged her to go with this, and see how she
felt when she let her shoulders do this. After a few minutes,
she began to cry softly, putting her face in her hands and
slumping over in her chair. When she finished, she re-
counted a memory of being about eight years old, cringing
in front of her father who was yelling and had his hand
raised to slap her in the face. She had been trying to protect her face by hunching her shoulders. Remembering this
incident allowed her to cry more deeply—which she did
for about ten minutes. When she was finally quiet, we
stood and hugged for a long time.

We sat back down then, and I asked her if the confron-
tation with her boss felt in any way related to her memory.
She said yes—that it was almost impossible for her to take
criticism from anyone, that it always felt like she was back
with her father, about to be hit. When I asked her how

frequently that criticized feeling occurred, she said, "Often."

I said, "Does that mean you also mess up often?"

Again, her eyes got wide, and she snarled at me, "There you go again!" But this time, she was able to laugh. I remarked that her shoulders had become more relaxed-looking, and we ended the session with a few minutes of deep breathing to help her to feel the change in her body. In subsequent sessions, we were able to explore how she arranged to get criticized so that she could re-create the only feelings she ever felt familiar with, hurt and shame.

This is an example of a breakthrough session when working with a severely addicted person. It also illustrates how the principles of the Moving Cycle work. Within the Moving Cycle are five intentions and five interventions. The five intentions are:

1. To nurture
2. To support
3. To challenge
4. To reflect
5. To provide space

To nurture ourselves is to do for ourselves what, ideally, should have been done for us when we were born: to greet, affirm, welcome, and love ourselves. These elements are markedly missing in our interactions with the world when we are in the throes of abandoning direct experience. Nurturance is a basic need, and therapy can provide it in a very direct and embodied way. In the above session, I provided nurturance when I hugged her and when I listened to her true feelings.

Support is about being held, being joined, having a container in which our feelings can occur. A therapist can provide support when he or she allows us to have our feelings in an undistorted manner. When I kept my seat and did not take my client's anger at me personally, I was supporting her.

Challenging is an advanced skill. It requires the ability to cut through the bullshit without being aggressive or violent. In essence, the task is to not permit our clients or friends to practice their addictions in front of us. In the above case, I challenged the client's run-on story, which was the acting out of an addiction of being out of her body and into irresponsibility and denial. Challenging is a crucial move in the face of addictive processes.

Reflecting is like being a mirror. As therapists or friends, we feed back what we see and hear so that the person in front of us can see themselves accurately. The tricky part is that people almost never show us the whole picture. They present a partial mask—what they want us to see in order to get our approval. Our job then is to look deeply and to reflect back what they have hidden from us as well as what they are consciously showing us. Reflection has to do with accuracy, with perceiving the whole, without praise or blame, without distortion. My noting of her raised shoulders enabled my client to flesh out the whole picture of the experience she had gone through, accessing her ability to learn from it rather than have it be another repetition of the way things always were.

Last of all, providing space allows us to tolerate being in our own direct experience without a friend or therapist meddling. It often consists of simple silence. It has the effect of allowing us our own experience and providing a tangible feeling of being in charge of our own feelings. When I sat and waited for her to let me know how she was feeling, I provided space for her to find her own way into her essence.

The five interventions are:

1. To repeat
2. To contrast
3. To intensify
4. To specify
5. To generalize

These five interventions are in-the-moment therapeutic behaviors that accelerate our progress through the Moving Cycle. First, I can ask a client to repeat. This simply allows them to wake up to what they were already doing unconsciously. By my asking my client to repeat her shoulder hunching, she was able to investigate it.

Contrasting means to do the opposite. Movement tags are often an attempt to get away from something. By making a contrasting move, we can go toward that which we were avoiding. An example might be a tag I used to have of squeezing my index finger against my thumb. When I did the opposite—stretched those two fingers apart—I contacted a startled fear feeling, similar to the one we might get when we put our hands up to fend off an attack.

Intensification is like turning up the volume on our inner stereo so that we can hear the words to the music. With the above client, I asked her to intensify her shoulder hunching. By doing this, she could hear what a deeper part of herself was saying. When we intensify something, we can make it louder, so that we can't mistake the message it brings.

Generalizing is the act of applying an experience to the whole that was typically confined to a part. In the body, it can look like letting a slight squeeze of the eyes generalize into a squeezing of the brow, the mouth, the fists, and the chest, so that we can really support the emotion that is motivating us. In the session above, generalizing took the form of verbally working an incident into the fabric of her addiction to shame and hurt.

Specifying is the other side of the coin of generalizing. At times, we feel things only in hazy, generalized ways, states that are vague and hard to describe. Specifying helps to get a focused picture of a feeling. It can look like my asking a client to show me with her hand what a general feeling is like. When I asked a client some months ago to show me with his hand what the feeling was like in his belly, he made a wave-like motion that then reminded him of being rocked in his mother's lap. This image helped him to contact tender feelings he had towards his girlfriend.

The five intentions and the five interventions form a coherent structure of techniques within which the Moving Cycle can occur. By keeping a body emphasis, they allow us to use current, spontaneous experiences to deepen our inner life, to light the path of self-exploration.

The challenge of recovery from drug addiction is to stay alive and not harm anyone else. As we progress toward life-affirming recovery, we confront another challenge, that of feeling happy. Gay and Kathlyn Hendricks call this our "upper limits problem." What keeps us in the life-limiting category is often not unresolved trauma but simply a belief that we are not supposed to get too happy, too successful, too excited, too aroused. It is typically our families and our cultures that teach us "how much" we can be. If, like me, you had the dubious distinction of being raised Roman Catholic, you most likely had a limit put on how sexual you can feel before something is wrong with it. It was definitely OK to be smart in my family, but it was not OK to be voluptuous. We often don't even realize we are limiting ourselves according to what we've been taught. We simply assume that this is the way the world works. We then practice addictions as a way to bring ourselves back down to familiar predetermined limits of energy and aliveness. If we follow the adage "Everything was going fine, then *this* happened. See? It just goes to show you . . . ," we are practicing an addiction to a life-limiting status quo. If we have a tendency to mess up just when everything was going right, ditto. If mysterious calamities occur just when we are feeling good, the same is true.

One of the most important distinctions a drug addict must learn to make is the difference between joy and oblivion. Getting high is reinforcing because, like fool's gold, it closely resembles joy. In our brains, joy causes the release of endorphins, those delicious chemicals that produce pleasant serenity. Addictive drugs suck out and deplete endorphins, sometimes causing permanent damage to the brain's ability to ever produce more. For long-term addicts, it may take years to reestablish healthy production of endorphins, which is probably why recovery for these folks is so fragile for so long. Addicts say that the thing they miss most is the feeling of the high. This is why it becomes so crucial for recovery to be seen not as just an abstinence from self-harm but as an affirmation of joy and the ability to be happy.

The Moving Cycle is designed for all the phases of recovery—from the jaws of death to the gates of heaven. It is patterned on the natural processes of the body and how it likes to operate optimally, thrumming with vibration. A full cycle can take three minutes or three years. We are all on many Moving Cycles at one time, each of them moving forward at its own pace, all interconnected with each other and our world.

Penetration and Absorption

Though we are born with either a male or a female body, we all contain within ourselves both masculine and feminine components—we all carry the ability and the longing both to penetrate and to absorb life. Carl Jung called the masculine principle in women *animus* and the feminine in men *anima*. Eastern philosophies speak of the male and female principles within each of us as yin and yang. The anatomy of the two sexes creates an apt metaphor for our basic life purposes, and these purposes are what drives the Moving Cycle.

One of our prime purposes is penetration. My thesaurus gives as its first synonym for penetrate "to get through physically." It is our job to see into, to imbed ourselves in, to fully penetrate life. We sometimes speak of eyes as penetrating, meaning that they can see into us, into our essence, behind our masks. When we penetrate an idea, we fully understand it. When we penetrate our lover, we literally put our bodies into theirs. We do this because life demands it. Life demands that we be in it. This is our purpose, to look deeply at life and to recognize it.

If we hold back from penetrating life, we impoverish ourselves and the world. We cannot be a lover in the world and a lover of the world. Like the male anatomy, penetration requires a certain firmness to happen—we focus and direct ourselves, we suffuse our bodies with energy in order to enter actively into life. If we are afraid or unwilling to penetrate, particularly with our senses, we limit our aliveness.

We also have a biological imperative to absorb life, to let it enter into us, and to let part of it become us. My thesaurus gives "to physically take in, or occupy complete attention" as a synonym for *absorb*. Absorption is accomplished first through the senses, by our willingness to allow sensation to become perception. In order to absorb, we must soften and allow ourselves to be permeated with life. Like the female anatomy, we open ourselves, we take in. If we are unwilling to absorb, we must rigidify to keep life out. We limit our aliveness by tensing and holding out against life. Life, however, demands that we let it in.

It can often be the case that we require the environment to do whatever we become unwilling to do ourselves. If we are unwilling to assert ourselves and penetrate, then life will be assigned the job of penetrator, and we will end up feeling literally screwed by it. If we are unwilling to absorb life, we will require it to soak up all our energy, and we will assume that life is draining us. We assign to life the tasks that we are unwilling to do in an immature effort to get it to take care of us, and then we blame it for being so one-sided.

The Moving Cycle restores our willingness both to penetrate and absorb life. It also helps us to relearn the penetrating and absorbing skills we have lost. It cultivates both these life purposes by reestablishing boundaries that are permeable to life.

In the Awareness phase, we recover sensation. Sensation requires two types of attention in order to be cultivated: focused attention and broad attention. At times, we need to focus very narrowly on one discrete thing. If my son takes a bad fall on his roller blades, for example, I don't attend to anything else but his body until I am sure he is OK. A form of meditation called concentration practice cultivates this type of attention. In concentration practice you look at the flame of a candle (or some other object) and practice focusing attention solely on it as much as possible. It is through this type of attention that we learn to penetrate, to see deeply into and understand things.

The other, broader type of attention requires us to let go of focus and attend to nothing in particular. This is the type of attention that I use when I am looking over a beautiful panorama. I let my senses drift across the entire landscape, drinking it in. I may want to use this form of attention when I am teaching my classes—when I want to get a sense of how the whole room is doing, not just individuals. There are meditation practices that cultivate this skill as well. This form of attention restores our absorptiveness, our ability to see life in its broad brush strokes, to have a comprehensive overview of it.

In the awareness phase, we reacquaint ourselves with attention and wake up to how our bodies have patterned us to limit penetration and absorption. Attention is both an active and receptive process. The Moving Cycle is not so much about hashing through life's vagaries, but in recovering lost skills and qualities. In the Awareness phase, we re-learn how to really wake up.

The Owning phase has its own absorptive and penetrating features. This phase is about deepening our relationship to what we are aware of, of actually dancing with sensation so that we spiral further into ourselves, and the selves of others. For this to occur, we must both actively dive in and receptively allow the depths of our experience to move and change us. One of the founding mothers of dance therapy, Mary Whitehouse, described this as both moving and being moved. When we move with what we feel, we are being fully responsible within it. We neither grasp it nor push it away. We optimize our relationship to life by being an agent of it.

Allowing ourselves to be moved relates to our receptive side. We embrace life by allowing ourselves to be changed by it, moved by it. We often say that certain people or events move us to tears or laughter. Emotions are actually designed as short term change agents—they move us from one state to another, in an adaption to a spontaneous change in the environment. By allowing this to happen, we stay in responsive and responsible relationship to ourselves and the world.

We call people crazy who cannot seem either to move or be moved. We call them catatonic or depressed for not moving, and we call them antisocial or autistic for not being moved. If we make a habit out of oscillating between both extremes, we again loose our permeable relationship to life.

In the Acceptance phase, permeability has to do with the ability to love. By our fully feeling our feelings, they are allowed their transient life span—the swell, the crest, and the diminishing—which creates the space in which we can love and be loved. In this phase I like clients to work with the idea of being visible to themselves and others. In a session with one couple the husband became exasperated and yelled at his wife, "I don't feel *seen* by you!"

I then calmly asked him, "But are you allowing yourself to be visible?" This reframed the issue so we could look at his habits of withholding as well as her habits of inattention as co-creating the not-being-seen dynamic.

In the Acceptance phase the depths of who and where we are become visible. The shade rolls up on the window. In order for this increased visibility to be of use, love needs to both come in by and go out the window. In other words, love light beams both into us and from us. Can we let the love of the world in? Can we absorb the caring and affection of others? Can we also reveal our love to others? Can we direct a penetrating beam of love out to our favorite target? Love is the resetter of our upper-limits thermostat. It dissolves our rationales and excuses for limiting love.

When we get to the Action phase, we are ready for a new set of penetrating and absorptive skills. We apply assertion and reception in our daily lives, thus influencing and moving both ourselves and the world. We engage in opportunities and experiences that fine-tune our permeability and exercise it. We give our permeability a real context and purpose. We raise our children, we do our work, we love our families. When we become permeable creatures, life is elevated and human evolution moves in a positive direction. Action is very practical. It gets the dishes washed and the world fed. As we dance with assertive action and receptive action, we ourselves become agents of change, agents of life.

In the next section of the book, we will look at the specifics of using the body to reclaim a full and vibrant life. We can use many handy elements to promote the Moving Cycle. They can take the form of a walk in the woods as well as a therapy session; cooking dinner as well as taking a meditation class. It is in the quality of attention, in the response, in the commitment, in the action, that we can use all the material of our lives in the service of our evolution as human beings. Rumi is also credited with asking, "Do you pay regular visits to yourself?" By moving ourselves along the cycle of life, we can't help but pay constant calls on our essential selves.

Part Two

Reembodying Recovery

Specific Strategies of the Moving Cycle

5

Awareness as the Ground

*Attention or conscious concentration on almost
any part of the body produces some direct physical
effect on it.* —CHARLES DARWIN

Awareness is a focusing of attention, a commitment to
being in the present moment, an alertness. Our bodies
house nervous systems that do the job of receiving stimuli,
interpreting them, and organizing meaningful responses.
Our nervous systems are divided into two categories: autonomic and volitional. The autonomic nervous system re-
sponds automatically, predictably, and habitually to recurring events. Because of it, we don't have to think
consciously about breathing, digesting, or reflexive actions. If we had to think about all those actions we simply
wouldn't have time for anything else. Our volitional nervous system is designed to respond to new, unpredictable,
and ever-changing events. By not behaving in a fixed way
we can problem-solve, adapt quickly, and be creative. As
we go up the evolutionary scale, we could say that creatures progress from having almost no volitional nervous
system (like slugs) to those who have a tremendous capacity for spontaneous action and reflection, like humans. It
is accurate to say, though, that we all need both fixed programs and spontaneous ones.

Our life is comprised of a constant dance between habit and impulse. All creatures inherit a certain amount of fixed programming as part of their genetic heritage. The further we go up the evolutionary scale, though, the less fixed programming is genetically inherited and the more it is learned and imprinted through early childhood experience. Most animals are born fearing fire. Humans must learn to fear it. This human capacity to use direct experience to know something is what makes us so adaptable and creative. It also underlines the tremendous influence our early upbringing has on our behavior. Our early experiences can influence not only what we habituate to, but also the amount of habituation with which we operate. Some of us habitually limit our awareness, passing flowers and beautiful sunsets by, while others of us luxuriate in the sensory experience, merely for the sake of doing it.

Awareness is one of the first and most primal mechanisms that are shaped during our early years. We are born with sensory systems—eyes, ears, noses, skin, tongues—that have certain perceptual limits (we can see better than sharks, for example, but not as well as eagles). Furthermore, we have a biological survival need to sort out what is important at any one moment from what is extraneous. This mechanism is called the figure/ground relationship. It is our propensity to make certain perceptions move into the foreground and others into the background. If a snarling tiger is in front of us, we will give all our attention to that and not pay attention to the smell of jasmine on the breeze. If a lover strokes our arm, we will feel that and not the pressure of our bottom against the chair. We can only pay attention to one thing at a time, even though many things are going on. As humans, our early experiences largely determine what we consider important and therefore pay attention to at any one moment.

From a bodily perspective, we can define the physical unconscious as the sensations that we aren't perceiving, aren't engaging with. And just like the traditional mental model of the unconscious, the physical unconscious is a rich source of information, memory, and repressed life. Our physical unconscious is accessible through the Awareness phase. We learn to focus our attention toward that which we have habitually kept out of our attention field. We have been used to defining ourselves through what we are used to paying attention to. By becoming willing to attend to anything that our senses can perceive, we expand ourselves, increasing our adaptiveness and enriching the world.

Early events, families, religion, and culture all have a stake in shaping our awareness so that it fits into existing systems of thought and behavior. Human systems are designed to provide and transmit the necessary automatic habits that ensure our survival. The transmission of these systems is one of the primary functions of parenting: we must teach our children how the world works, because they have insufficient genetic programming to know it themselves. It is also one of our primary functions as parents to preserve and nurture our children's capability for behaving creatively. Children become dysfunctional adults when they have been either overly programmed or given insufficient care and guidance to form healthy habits. This is the basis of addiction. Families, societies, and random events shape what we pay attention to and even the amount of free attention we have.

I notice attentional habits frequently when I do couples work. The wife's childhood training has been focused on learning to do things right, on being an obedient child, and on listening to her parents' constant criticisms of her. The husband may have had a childhood where he was largely ignored and told to go play in his room a lot. As adults, both have attentional habits that revolve around this training. She assumes she will be criticized for everything she does; he assumes his efforts will be ignored. They both put up what is called listening shields, and they literally can't see the moments when their spouse is not behaving according to their expected programming. They only see that which is consonant with their fixed attentional programming.

When an event occurs, it impacts on our senses, causing the stimulation of our nervous system. We can either pay attention to or ignore this stimulus. We absolutely will pay attention to it if it affects our survival. We will also pay attention when we are motivated—like by the smell of food when we are hungry. Beyond survival and motivation, we will make things figural if we are interested in them. We are pretty much already wired at birth for many survival issues. This is because most of what is threatening to one person is also threatening to another, so we can afford to have some fixed programming here. Motivation is also largely determined by common biological forces (like hunger and thirst) but it is individually manifested. Differences in our structure and functioning will affect things like when we get hungry, at what temperature we will get cold, and so forth. Our early environment will shape these differences. Interest, on the other hand, is largely determined by our unique makeup and our early learning experiences. Our formative history will guide us toward savoring certain experiences and shrinking away from others. One family will teach its children to repress or ignore sexual feelings, another will help their children celebrate them. Some cultures impose belief systems that shrink the aliveness of women, others celebrate their women. We can even say that some families and cultures have a more "shrinking" orientation to life, while others are more "savoring." It is my experience that addiction is rooted in a shrinking orientation toward awareness and aliveness. This is because we have a basic biological need for lots of interest in and curiosity about our world. If this need is interfered with, we will experience the pain of need deprivation and will attempt to assuage this pain and feel a substitute gratification.

How does this early environmental shaping occur? If we remember figure 4, the Grids of Meaning diagram (see page 66), we can see that early experiences can shape whether or not we choose to interpret or reflect information, whether we habituate to judging or including, controlling or responding.

We start with an event. Let's say Fred and Joe are driving their cars, there is a red light ahead of them, and they both stop for it. Fred stops, and registers that he is at a stop light and notices the traffic and then the music on the radio. He is *describing* his experience to himself, and he is relating to it openly and with curiosity. He begins to sing to the music, and sway to it slightly, keeping his eye on the light. He is *reflecting* with his experience the way it is. He feels good. The song reminds him of an incident that he wants to tell his wife. He is *including* himself and the song and his wife in a *responsive action* that results from his going with his experience. Fred can do this because he had a childhood that allowed him to be curious, responsive, and open to his world attentionally. He received parenting that reinforced his relating to the present moment, more than fussing with controlling how the world *should* be.

Joe, on the other hand, stops at the light and fumes. It is because of this red light that he will be late for work. He is *interpreting* his experience, assigning it a meaning. He does not like to be late for work, and he is mad that this is happening to him. He is assigning a value to his experience, *judging* it to be wrong and bad. If something is bad, he must work to change it. He has an *urge to control* his experience and resolves to call up the city managers and give them an earful about the timing of their lousy lights. It is likely that Joe's childhood was organized around paying attention to restrictive grids of meaning with which he must constantly compare his current experience. If his current experience doesn't match what he was taught about how the world should work, he will spend more time fussing over the differences between the experience he is having versus the experience he is supposed to have. This takes up a lot of his time and energy. Regardless of whether it is seen through Joe's filters or Fred's filters, the red light is the same, impartially doing its thing in the world.

In the first scenario, whatever arises is allowed to be experienced as it is. By simply taking it in and being with it, we can have a rich and rewarding experience, even at a red light. In the second instance, we shrink away from what is and vote for a self-absorbed scenario that requires wrongness and results in an attempt to control. The attempt to control is the modus operandi of addiction.

Our families and cultures give us many lessons about when it is OK to "go with" an experience and when it is imperative to interpret and control it. We are literally conditioned to interpret and judge. Racism and sexism are two classic examples of conditioned kinds of judgment. We are taught to interpret skin color or gender as having certain properties which are judged to be good or bad. We then have to control the people with the offending characteristics, subjugate them. The conditioning can also cause us to judge things as good: if *Catholic* is good, then *Jewish* may be judged as bad, for example. When someone is right, that always means someone else somewhere is wrong. If something is good, then our urge to control manifests as a need to keep that good thing from going away. We will vote to keep eating the chocolate cake instead of going with the fact that our stomach is full and aching. Addiction is the process of shrinking from our awareness and interpreting, judging, and attempting to control our experience.

What we need is a Witness—to reclaim our curiosity, our openness, our awakeness to life, we need to reclaim our ability to experience the world as it is. A witness is someone who is present, who observes. We all are born with the ability to witness, and for some of us this ability is savored, while for others it is closed down. Wherever we close down our own ability to witness in our lives, we will practice an addiction.

Most spiritual traditions have some mechanism for developing the Witness. Perhaps this is why many people in the addictions field stress spirituality as a part of recovery—with its mechanisms that include contemplation, meditation, and prayer. All of these enhance our ability to witness the world. Meditation is specifically designed to help us shift our figure/ground relationship so that we are not paying attention to our thoughts but to the pure state of being awake, separate from the contents of what we are aware of. Sam Keen (1983, 140) put it well when he stated:

The cure for addiction lies in developing the witness self. When I pause in the presence of my grasping need and do not take a fix, I become capable of surveying a larger field of my desires; then I can decide freely which I will satisfy. . . . The illusion of addiction depends upon keeping the multiplicity of our desires unconscious. When I invite all that I am into awareness I realize that no one substance, activity, or person has the capacity to satisfy me fully. I leave aside the security of the fix and begin the adventure of falling in love with the multiplicity of the self and the world.

Awareness in the Body

The Witness is crucial on a body level. Our first experience as infants is physical. The first things we are taught that it is OK to pay attention to involve our bodies. The first strategies we use to modulate our attention are through the body. And our first recovery can also be in the body. What is it that we recover in our bodies? We recover sensation, breath, and movement.

Sensations are the ingredients of the soup of our experience. We actually know we are angry because we feel the tension in our jaw, the clench in our fist. We are thrilled with a rose because we smell its fragrance, we experience its rich color and texture. I wish I had a nickel for every time I asked a recovering client what they were feeling and the answer I got was "I don't know" or "OK, I suppose." When I would ask for sensations, I would get "Nothing" or "Fine." What I have noticed is that most people in the throes of addiction have so compromised their sensory system that it takes major pain or pleasure to register anything. I often ask, "Do you feel the pressure of your bottom on the chair?" or "Do you feel your breath going in and out?" The answer is usually a yes, with a "So what?"

attitude. Sensation as simply an experience of aliveness has been lost, and they have opted instead for registering only things which are bad and should be avoided, or good and should be sought out.

Tensing up or becoming depressed are two ways to inhibit sensation. They are also our best strategies for inhibiting movement. Tension results from movement that is held back in the body. Flaccidity, or limpness, is movement that is depressed. The next time you get tense in your shoulders (which carry the muscles for arm movement), ask yourself if there is anyone or anything you'd like to punch out, or reach for, or hold. The next time you feel collapsed in your chest, reestablish your breath through there and open up to what sensations or emotions you may have been avoiding. Movement, sensation, and breath are the offspring of aliveness. They can form the basis of curiosity, responsiveness, openness, and participation with life. They are the component parts of awareness, and can be the fuel for the journey of recovering ourselves.

We are not very good at finding things in the dark. When the lights are out, we may accidently stumble onto (or into) things; this is a random and sometimes painful process. What we need to do is turn the lights on. Awareness is the act of turning on our inner lights and focusing on what they illumine in such a way that we can see what we want and where to go. The first place to direct the light is to our bodies.

Cognitive Awareness

Our thoughts as well as our bodies are subject to attentional habits. By working with our cognitive awareness, we can undo patterns of attention that set us up to see the world and ourselves a certain way. The first way to work with our thoughts is to simply witness that we are thinking. By developing the ability to note that right now we are thinking (regardless of what the thoughts are about) we can restore our ability to choose our state of consciousness. I worked with a couple who were stuck in a dynamic of blaming each other for their lack of connection and intimacy. I noticed that at opportune moments, they each had cognitive distraction strategies that avoided closeness. She would get very focused on what he was or wasn't doing right. He would go into his head and try to think of explanations for why things were occurring.

At a pivotal opportunity point in one session, I asked the husband if he really *wanted* to be thinking right now. He didn't understand my question. I told him that he also had the option of feeling as well as thinking—I asked him what he was feeling. After a bit of exploration he realized he was scared, and he was able to talk about his feeling to his wife. I turned to the wife and asked if she would be willing to pay more attention to what her experience was, noting her tendency at this point to pay attention to her husband instead. When she focused her attention differently, on herself, she was able to share herself. Making these attentional shifts provided a breakthrough for them both.

The husband had an attentional pattern of going into his head and thinking out of fear of intimacy. I have noticed that it is a waste of therapeutic time to attend to and analyze the contents of what someone is thinking when the issue at hand is that the person is using thinking itself as a defense strategy. The wife employed an attentional pattern of focusing outside of herself right when she needed to be sharing herself in order to create intimacy. It would have been a waste of therapeutic time to discuss and analyze her perceptions of her husband when it was the act of focusing externally that was getting her in trouble.

The Awareness phase of the Moving Cycle cultivates our waking up to our patterns of attention and making conscious choices to focus our attention into previously unilluminated places in ourselves. There is a great story that illustrates this principle: On a darkened street, a man was on his hands and knees, searching for something in the light of the street lamp. Another man came along and asked him what he was doing. "Why, I'm searching for my car keys, of course." he replied.

"Where did you lose them?" the other man asked.

The first man pointed across the street, "Over there."

"Well, why don't you look over there?" the inquiring man asked.

"Because this is where the light is!" he answered.

Clients tend to come into therapy aware of something that is wrong, which they want therapy to fix. Their light is focused on that side of the street, and they are very aware of this thing that is wrong. They are not aware, however, of the parts of themselves that they were taught to ignore. These parts have withered and are what is actually creating the problem. Attention is like sunlight and water—whatever you apply it to will grow. If you attend to the red light as a problem, it becomes more and more of one.

As a therapist, I am hired to witness the whole client, not just the parts they consciously present to me—and usually what they would like me to see is what they think will get them the love and approval the need. I am hired to help them focus the light unconditionally on any and all parts of themselves. My being an external witness sets the stage for the development of their own internal witness. One of my jobs is to unconditionally bathe them with my attention, so that they can undo the woundedness of a history that told them some parts of themselves were acceptable and some weren't. It is when a client can witness and appreciate everything that comes into their awareness that I know it is time to terminate therapy.

In order to be able to work with an attentional thinking pattern, we must first witness how and what we pay attention to; we work with the process of attending more than the content. As I stated before, we can become addicted to switching to thinking and ignoring feeling. Another pattern is that we can habitually think about something so much that we think the thought is real. If we don't attend to the raw data of experience, we make our thoughts seem real because we pay attention only to them. If I think that people are out to get me, that is what I will be alert for, that is what I will see. This is how our loved ones end up looking like our family of origin—it is because we only attend to aspects of them that conform to our existing perceptual patterns.

Identifying patterns of attention can be tricky at first. We must shift awareness from the contents to the process by asking ourselves different kinds of questions, such as these:

- Which of my senses do I favor? Do I focus more on sight, hearing, or touch?
- What kinds of things draw my attention?
- What kinds of things do I get bored with?
- When things get upsetting, where does my attention go?
- When things get pleasurable, where does my attention go?

- When my attention wanders, where does it go? Do I plan, do I reminisce? Do I space out?
- Under what kinds of circumstances do I find it hard to stay focused?
- What do I find myself thinking about over and over? What assumptions about the world does this lead to?
- What parts of my body am I more aware of? Less aware of?
- Do I have a tendency to spend a lot of my time focused on what is going on outside of me, or maybe inside of me?

As we ask ourselves these questions, we gather a new kind of information that makes new options possible. The practices of the Awareness phase are ones that broaden our range of incoming sensation and of ongoing thinking. We can oscillate between focused and broad attention, we can think about other options, we can attend directly to the comings and goings of life, perceiving it not through the eyes of our ancestors but through our own senses.

There are many practices that cultivate awareness that have been around for a long time and that are very simple to do. I notice that I need a broad range of attentional activities, ones that feed different aspects of my nature. For all parts of myself, I meditate. For my body, I do t'ai chi and I dance. For my energy and emotions, I practice various breathwork disciplines. For my thoughts, I practice oscillating my attention—particularly in nature. And I paint. Engaging in creative acts is crucial for awareness discipline. What serves me best are activities that incorporate all aspects of myself, such as meditative walks in deep wilderness. I have found that sea kayaking and canoeing are also excellent contemplative forms.

I find that I need to fuel my awareness each and every

day. I always choose meditation, and beyond that I let myself lean toward other activities toward which I am naturally drawn. I also find that I need periods of deep retreat
into attentional practices. At least three times a year, I trek
into the wilderness. At least once a year, I go on an extended meditation retreat. By commiting to these practices, by making them as necessary to me as my breath, I
find I have tremendous amounts of energy, energy which
can be spent creating, assisting, producing.

Below are a few exercises to promote and enhance
awareness, beginning with physical sensation. They are designed to help us map the territory of awakeness so that
we can begin the journey toward a more life-promoting
kind of existence. They can also help us focus toward
choosing various awareness practices that locate us, that
bring us home, that sit us down at the feast on life's table.

Exercises for the Awareness Phase

1. Take a moment to put your attention inside yourself
and describe the physical sensations in your body, free of
any interpretation or judgment. If you start judging yourself, simply note that you are judging yourself and go back
to the sensations. Some sensations may be very subtle.
That's fine—no sensation is any more important than any
other right now. Even the feeling that nothing is going on
is a feeling. Scan your body and pay attention to every part
of it, every nook and cranny. Notice which parts dominate
your attention and which don't seem to feel anything.
Each time you become aware of some body sensation,
breathe deeply and say to yourself, "Now I am aware
that. . . ." Alternately tense and relax your body parts, and
describe your experience of them to yourself. Notice where
it was easy to attend and where it was more difficult.

2. Take a few moments to sit and breathe deeply. On the inbreath, focus on getting the breath all the way down into your belly. If you have trouble getting your belly to expand, you might want to try this lying down first. On the outbreath, focus on letting go of as many muscle groups as you can so that the air can just fall out. Exhale with your mouth slightly open. If you have trouble exhaling this way, try sighing audibly as the air falls out. Keep this up for a few minutes. If you feel at all dizzy or lightheaded, stop the full breathing until it subsides, and then go back to it a few more times. Notice what emotions, sensations, or feelings come up. As you notice these, take this as a cue that that part of you wants more breath. Breathe more deeply into your tension, your sadness, your boredom, or your fluttery feelings. Let your attention rest lightly on them, and simply describe the feel of them to yourself. Stay curious, and don't try to find explanations or answers. It is as if you could greet each thing that arises in your attention, welcoming it in with your breath. Just keep breathing for breathing's sake.

3. Identify a part of your body that feels tense right now. Play with exaggerating the tension slightly. When you exaggerate it, what movement seems to want to develop? Let the movement happen, not trying to direct it, but simply following the tension so that it is expressed exactly the way it is. What does this movement become? How have you been restricting yourself from this movement lately?

4. Identify a lax, collapsed, or mushy part of your body. First, try exaggerating the quality of it. Does concentrating on it take you into some kind of body position? How might you characterize that position? For example, if you slump your chest more, do you feel like a hopelessly de-

pressed person? Does this characterization fit how you
have been operating in the world in some way? What results, both positive and negative, does this position get you
in your current environment? Make sure you look at the
advantages as well as the disadvantages of this position. If
you are willing to experiment with dropping that position,
put your full breathing in it. Stay with it, even when you
feel tired or spaced-out or finished. Make your breath
more important than the position. As you stay with it,
what feelings arise? How might you have been avoiding
these feelings? Let yourself feel them. Find the movement
that wants to occur when you allow yourself to feel this
feeling. This may take you up and around the room.

5. Focus on a repetitive gesture that you do, and do it
consciously. Notice how you feel as you give it your full
attention. You can play with it by exaggerating it, doing a
contrasting or opposing movement, repeating it, letting it
expand into other parts of your body, or letting it develop
into a purposeful and complete movement. What does the
movement become? What is that movement trying to say
to you? Is there any reason you might not want to listen to
this part of you? Allow yourself to do the complete movement very purposefully as many times during the day as
you want.

6. Put an object in front of you and look at it. See how
deeply you can perceive its qualities. Notice when you
make value judgments about its qualities and note them.
Assume that this is a way that you have learned to judge
yourself. Go back to the object. Let yourself touch it, listen
to it, taste it, just for a few minutes. Finish by turning your
attention inside, and looking just as deeply at what is
going on within you.

7. Practice oscillating your attention between what is

going on inside of you and what is going on in the environment. You may want to do this at first in a fairly neutral environment, like an outdoor setting. Notice if you have any tendencies to get caught for periods of time with your attention outside or inside. Just note it and go back to oscillating between inside and outside. Then practice oscillating your attention in more challenging circumstances, such as looking into a loved one's face. Notice what patterns you carry in the oscillations. The real benefit comes when you can practice oscillating attention while under stress, like a conflict with a friend. By attending to the oscillation during these times, you create a space for both of you to take care of yourself and your feelings, and also to perceive your friend directly, wearing fewer perceptual filters from the past.

8. Choose an activity that you like, that you find relaxing and that gently focuses your attention. It could be sewing, listening to music, taking a walk, or some kind of art making. Commit to at least a few minutes of this activity each day. TV does not count—it often acts as an addictive substitute for attentional nourishment.

9. Ask yourself what play means to you. How do you define it? How do you arrange for it in your daily life? One of the features of play is that it is done for no other reason than the pleasure of doing it. Are you playing enough? Watch others at play, especially children. What appeals to you about what they are doing? Do you notice any internal prohibitions against playing? Who would you choose as a play partner? Make a commitment to playing each day and see what kinds of opportunities this commitment creates.

6

Taking Responsibility Equals Taking Your Body Back

The most exhausting thing in life, I have
discovered, is being insincere.
                —ANNE MORROW LINDBERG,
                    A Gift from the Sea

The first responsibility is information, is truth.
                        —ADLAI STEVENSON

The second phase of the Moving Cycle is *Owning*. In Owning we deeply recover our creativity, our integrity, and our ability to problem-solve. Owning involves reclaiming our body's birthright of intuitive action, trusting that our body knows how to make healthy choices. In the Awareness phase, we identify and work with our habits. In the Owning phase, we identify and work with our choices.

Responsibility's other name is the ability to respond. It means that if an event occurs, we are able to engage with it rather than retreat from it. It starts with our ability to be aware that the event is occurring, and proceeds with our ability to move with the event and to be moved by it. We not only identify that we are angry, but we let ourselves feel it. When we respond, we are allowing ourselves to shape and be shaped by life, to both penetrate it and absorb it by remaining in active relationship to it. If life has dealt us abuse or trauma, we tend to experience it as squashing us rather than shaping us, and we will fight responsive action on the habituated belief that we are about to get squashed. We do not believe that we are participants in the shaping of our lives. In order to prevent this anticipated flattening we squash ourselves in advance.

I call this anticipatory self-squashing "reacting." In contrast to responding, reacting is a process of fighting what is. It is a mix of what is happening now mixed up with all the unfinished woundings of the past. We have all experienced this: A loved one says, "You have some dirt on your chin," and we explode with, "How dare you treat me like a child! You are so critical and controlling! I don't know how I put up with you!" Clearly, this reaction is not about dirt on the chin but about all the times in the past when we were ever put down. The current event stimulates the unfinished wounding, and the wounding leaks or explodes out, riding on the back of the current event, polluting it, making it not a current event but a recapitulation of what was before. Reaction is a process of being out of proportion to the event that stimulates it.

Reaction usually involves some kind of withdrawal or contraction in the body. Response involves some kind of opening and readiness in the body. Reaction is a defensive action that results from losing our boundaries—we are literally invaded by the old patterns of behavior. In response, we get our boundaries back—we discriminate between what was in the past, what might be in the future, and what is now. This is how we can begin to tell the difference between the two. Reaction is, from this standpoint, not a negative or bad experience. It is simply our inner self rais-

ing its hand and saying, "Hey! I need some healing here!"
It heralds an opportunity for transformation. By turning
our awareness to our bodies and distinguishing between
response and reaction we find our way home—back to our
first and primal home, our body.

We each have individual patterns for responding and reacting. I have a tendency to tighten my jaw and the muscles around my eyes when I react. Many people alter and
limit their breathing. The Owning phase is about finding
our reactive habits and working with them consciously.
Reacting often involves a movement tag, a subtle gesture
that is like a marker of unfinished wounding. The task of
the Owning phase is to commit to shifting a reactive habit
into a conscious action. In this way we access our ability
to respond to an event, dance with it, complete it.

What occurs when we vote for participating with an old
wound instead of rejecting, projecting, and controlling it
is that we lay it to rest. Our need to keep reasserting it,
reliving it, attracting it disappears. The part of us that constructed an elaborate defense around it actually dies. Clients within the depths of the Owning phase will often report a feeling of impending death, and this can actually be
quite an accurate feeling. They *are* dying. The part of them
that had to construct an identity, a belief system, and a
strategy around this old wound will cease to have any need
to live. In the Owning phase, one of our most powerful
experiences is allowing that part of ourselves to die.

How do we accomplish this conscious death? We do it
by keeping our attention on our current, direct experience,
and by telling the truth about it. Telling the truth is an
extremely potent and efficient tool for healing addiction,
for locating home. Because it is a statement of what is, it
aligns us with our essence and enables us to act from our

essence. It is one of the most life-affirming things we can do, and as such it unravels the death-affirmation that addiction creates. Often the strategy for maintaining the addiction is so ingrained in us that we don't know the truth when we see it. We need to relearn what the truth is and how to tell it. Here are some characteristics of the truth:

- It is descriptive rather than interpretive: "I tend to space out when you are talking," rather than "You are boring when you talk."
- It is a statement about yourself: "I feel frightened," or "I was angry with you yesterday."
- It is a statement of your process rather than your position: "My hands are clammy," or "I want to go away right now," rather than "You make me sick."
- It is unarguable: "There is a fluttering in my stomach," rather than "You always put me down."
- It is nonjudgmental: "I get scared every time I talk about this," rather than "I'm just a scaredy-cat and a wimp around this issue."
- It is based in direct experience: "When I see you I get a tingle in my chest," rather than "This is about my lingering issues with my mother."
- It resonates in our bodies in an exciting and satisfying way: "I feel such a sense of relief now that I've told you about my affair. I'm shaking all over and I'm scared, and I am also breathing fully for the first time in months."

Here is a list of what the truth is *not:*

- It is not a statement about someone else: "What you did was wrong," or "You make me angry."
- It is not a fixed assessment: "I am a bad person," or "I am right."
- It is not an opinion or value judgment: "You are angry with me," or "What you did was mean and despicable."
- It is not secondhand: "She told me you don't like me."

Telling the truth generates a lot of energy, both in ourselves and in the people with whom we share it. Energy is
generated each time we align ourselves with our essence.
Often we withhold the truth because we are not used to
that much energy, and we think we cannot handle it, or
because we think that whoever we might tell it to might
not be able to handle the intense aliveness that it generates.
Both of these codependent assumptions are based on early
experiences that taught us that if we assert ourselves we
will be left, we will be bad, we will be punished, that there
won't be enough. Also, if we don't know how to tell the
truth and we learn to indulge in untrue statements like the
above, we will associate truth with pain. The non-truths
above are all designed to hurt. If that is what the truth is,
then we won't want any part of it.

The reality is that if we follow our body's cues, the energy created by telling the truth will be completely friendly
and transformative. This was illustrated to me by a client
who was experiencing an attraction to a man at work. She
was withholding this information from her husband because she felt it would only hurt and upset him. Since she
wasn't going to act on her attraction, what harm was there
in this little secret? She didn't want to talk about it. What
she did want to talk about was the lack of sexual feeling
toward her husband that had been surfacing for her lately.
When I suggested that there might be a relationship between these two things she at first became very defensive.
She was very fearful that there *was* a relationship between
her feelings for these two men. When she followed the
tightening in her stomach that this fear produced she could
hear her mother's voice telling her as a young child not to
touch herself. Her mother told her that no man would
want to marry her if he found out she touched herself. As

she stayed with this feeling and completed it by allowing the shaking movements in her torso free rein, she realized that she had internalized this event. She "got it" that she assumed her sexuality was bad, and she had projected this onto her husband. She went home and told her husband everything. Her honesty broke a log jam of feelings they both had been suppressing. As they revealed themselves to each other, they experienced an excitement for each other that they hadn't had since they were newlyweds. My client phoned me in a few days to let me know that she and her husband had decided that telling the truth was one of the sexiest things they had ever done.

There comes a point in any experience when we can tell the truth about it or retreat from it. Here are some of the things we do when we are at the opportunity point for telling the truth and we hover toward our addictive process instead:

- We get stupid. All of a sudden we don't know what is going on or how we feel.
- We get intellectual. We try to get away with not being genuine by analyzing the situation, often accurately and brilliantly.
- We make excuses. We find reasons that seem legitimate for not telling it like it is.
- We get depressed or hopeless. We assume that it's too hard, too futile, or we just can't do it.
- We don't take responsibility. We decide it's someone else's problem or fault. They have to change, not us.
- We get controlling. We can do this by setting conditions for telling the truth ("I will if you will"), by withholding it until we are in control, or by using an emotion like anger or kindness to manipulate someone else into doing it for us.

• We ask questions instead of making statements. We suddenly want to know how the *other* person feels.

All of these strategies are ways in which we strike deals in order to limit our energy and aliveness in exchange for protection against the positive energy or feelings of lack that telling the truth will reveal. This may have been necessary in our childhood, but as adults, this bargain only causes pain, numbness, and dysfunction.

Sometimes it can take a few steps to get to our deepest truth. This is because the truth often reveals itself to us in layers, one statement deepening into the next. As we get closer and closer to the core of our being through accurate description, we can feel a tremendous vibratory shift in our body that signals we have arrived, that we have accessed our essence and are occupying it. The vibration is our aliveness returning, our bodysong that rejoices in the knowing that it is OK to be all here—every microscopic part of us.

The following transcript from a session with a client illustrates the principle of returning to the truth in layers. The client, Sue, had come in complaining about her on-again, off-again relationship with her boyfriend. He had come over the other night, and they had fought. Her complaint centered around her boyfriend's not wanting to commit to being monogamous with her.

CHRISTINE: I notice that when you talk about the fight, you make a wavy motion with your hands. Go ahead and just do that motion for a minute.

SUE: (*Waves her hands*) I feel rattled.

CHRISTINE: The fight rattled you?

SUE: Yes. He just won't see how immature he is being.

CHRISTINE: Just let yourself be rattled for a minute. Just be with that feeling.

SUE: (*Closes her eyes, lets her body shake*) I feel like I could just shake him, shake some sense into him.

CHRISTINE: Keep going with the shaking. I notice your hands are beginning to clench too.

SUE: (*Clenching her hands into fists*) If he only knew how much this hurts, how much he is hurting me.

CHRISTINE: Put your attention back to your hands. What do they want to do now?

SUE: (*Clenched hands go to her throat in a choking gesture*) I feel like I'm going to suffocate. It feels like I'm scared.

CHRISTINE: Okay, stay with that feeling. Does the fear remind you of anything?

SUE: (*Begins to cry*) It happens all the time with him.

CHRISTINE: When was the first time you remember feeling this feeling?

SUE: When I was a kid (*A minute or two elapses while she cries*)

CHRISTINE: What is the memory?

SUE: My father yelling at my mother, telling her that if she was going to act like a bitch he was going to go out. Then he would storm out of the house and my mom would cry.

CHRISTINE: And you would be scared when that happened?

SUE: Yeah, I'd hide behind the couch.

CHRISTINE: What do you feel in your body now?

SUE: A collapsing feeling in my chest. Like I'm giving up.

CHRISTINE: Does that feel familiar?

SUE: Yeah (*she smiles wryly*). I feel alternately angry and like giving up with my boyfriend.

CHRISTINE: What do you want with your boyfriend?

SUE: I want him to stay home! (*clenches her hands*)

CHRISTINE: Like your Mom wanted your Dad . . .

SUE: (*In tears*) Yeah.

CHRISTINE: How did your Mom relate to your Dad around this issue?

SUE: (*Quiet for a minute*) It seemed like she would get nervous after dinner, get edgy. She'd ask him in this sarcastic voice if he was going to go out. Then the fight would start. (*Several moments of silence*) Sounds like I'm playing this out again, doesn't it?

CHRISTINE: Yup.

SUE: I don't want to be my mother! She was always unhappy, always complaining about being alone.

CHRISTINE: Close your eyes now and put your attention inside. What do you notice?

SUE: (*After some time*) I notice an ache in my chest. Like my heart aches.

CHRISTINE: So feeling your heart and having it ache go together?

SUE: (*Laughs*) Yeah.

The rest of the session was spent talking about her inheritance of her parents' brokenheartedness. We designed an exercise where she would attend to her heart and note when she might be experiencing moments that did not fit into the brokenhearted pattern. This happened most notably when she was with her dog, whom she loved and by whom she felt completely loved. In subsequent sessions we played with the idea that she could treat her boyfriend like her dog (we had some fun with that). She began to notice the moments when she would begin to fear he would go away, and she worked on telling him the truth of her experience right then. She was able to articulate her fear and to tell him how much she realized that she was actually afraid of getting close to him. He told her about his fear of getting close as well. She reported that they were beginning to get closer just by doing that.

This is an example of finding one's way back to the truth. When life feels problematic, it is because we are somehow not in alignment with it. Finding our way back to where we deviated from the truth will help to locate us again. Sue was able to distinguish between her responses to the opportunity to get close to her boyfriend, and her reactions to her history. By tracking and expressing her direct experience, she located herself, rather than reenacting her parents' feelings.

One of the great side effects of telling the truth is that it restores our gracefulness. When we go with the flow of what is happening, it all gets a lot easier. When we experience our essence directly, we create grace in the world. We become capable of perceiving the essential grace in others. Grace in this sense is essence recognizing itself. We reclaim, in the Owning phase, the ability to apprehend and resonate with essence as it occurs in all things.

Recovering Integrity

Committing to the truth is a deeply transformational act. It awakens our integrity and our trust in ourselves and the world. It puts us back in the sacred realm of choice rather than the hellish hole of compulsion. When we begin to act more responsibly in our lives, we are in alignment with the way life operates. Integrity occurs. Integrity is an interesting word, because it means both a state of being whole, complete, having structural soundness, as well as an act of doing what we say we will do. This double meaning is no coincidence—one brings about the other. They occur in conjunction.

Integrity then, is a statement about our body's structure, about how it can operate cohesively. We break the cohesion of our bodies when we limit sensory nourishment, or when we control the types of sensory experiences we think we should have. We reestablish our physical cohesion through getting back to the raw data of experiencing what is happening here and now. We get our bodies back, and with our bodies back, we are capable of moving and being moved by life.

Emotional integrity is about letting a feeling be itself, from beginning to end. Emotions are transient phenomena. They come and they go. They are a surge of energy that corrects or finesses our alignment with what is happening. I remember once I was told by a friend that I was looking particularly beautiful. I flushed, held my breath, and began to say something negative. My friend called me on this. When I witnessed my experience, I realized the feeling I was having was embarrassment. The embarrassment was the measure of the energy it took to handle the experience I was having. What I was being told contradicted an old core belief I held of my "plainness." The feeling was the measure of the distance between these two points, and it was designed to help me reestablish a reality in which there was no distance between what I believed and what my experience was. I got that I didn't need to hold on to a limiting core belief of ugliness any longer. Though I also know that I don't look like the women on the cover of *Vogue,* I got that I could play with my definition of beauty, forming one that allowed me to feel the most alive and to support the aliveness of others.

In this case, the feeling of embarrassment was an energy event that gave me the fuel to transform, to get in more fine-tuned alignment with myself and the world. If I take the opportunity the feeling presents, then I get the goodies it brings. If I skip the opportunity, the feeling, the emotion is experienced as threatening to the status quo. I won't want to feel the feeling, and I will addict to doing whatever it takes to keep the feeling at bay. In the process, I lose my emotional integrity, my ability to let feelings reestablish my wholeness. My feelings become feared and, paradoxically, they will keep reasserting themselves. Feelings are intended to move us, and until they move us toward a higher level of organization, they will persist. So that which you keep feeling is that which you haven't let yourself feel completely.

Emotions are evolution on the spot. They suffuse our systems with the energy to transform, to mutate into the life form we most wish to be and are meant to be. They locate our experience, they shake us up, and the shaking rearranges things into a more perfect union.

Integrity is a process of thought as well. Just as knowing who we are seems like a vastly overrated state, so does holding fixed beliefs. Our whole species seems to get into the most trouble when we believe our beliefs are reality in its absolute form. Absolutism requires that anyone who doesn't believe the way we do is wrong. And from that point control and violence arise. Absolutism is making our beliefs more important, more real, than our experience. This negating of the world is an all too familiar way to start a war. Like our cells, beliefs seem to operate best when they are permeable. Another way to put it is that our beliefs need *utility*.

A belief has integrity when it represents what is really happening. In this way it has a usefulness, a utility in the world. I used to believe that men were never there when you needed them. This belief, though inaccurate, had a lot of utility in my childhood, for it helped me feel closer to my mother, who shared the belief with me. Our shared belief created a bond that I needed. Of course, as an adult I found that this belief had outlived its usefulness through repeated attempts to make the world look that way when it didn't. I suffered, and put several men in my life through suffering, until I got willing to allow my current experiences to form my beliefs rather than to let them be formed by my need to be close to my mother. I changed my beliefs in order to increase their utility in my life. In this way, beliefs work for us rather than run us.

One of the most damaging things we can do to children is force them into our beliefs, telling them that they must operate the way we do instead of the way they do. When we give them the message that beliefs come from somewhere on high rather than from direct experience, we create a situation of moral deprivation in them.

Cognitive integrity, which gets worked on in the Owning phase of the Moving Cycle, reestablishes the integrity and utility of belief. Belief is a proclamation of the current situation, the present configuration. In the Owning phase, we stay with a direct experience completely, until it has a chance to completely penetrate us, and we have a chance to penetrate it. We also absorb it, and it is absorbed by us.

I once worked with a client who had been beaten as a child whenever he made even the slightest mistake. As an adult in therapy, it took him a while to even be able to articulate his core belief that the world is hostile and mean. In one session he was attributing a problem at work to a grumpy coworker. I asked him how he knew the man was grumpy. It took him a while, but he realized that he assumed this because the man had a habit of frowning at him. He assumed the man disapproved of his performance. When he went to work the next day, he checked this out with the coworker. The coworker was surprised; he didn't realize he was frowning when he saw my client. As they explored it, they found that the coworker would frown whenever my client got what he described as a pained look on his face. His frown was actually a worried frown. In subsequent sessions, my client was able to uncover a memory of the look on his father's face right before the beatings would happen.

One way that we vote to operate on our core beliefs instead of our direct experience is in situations where we don't have enough information. Our minds need fresh oxygen and glucose constantly, or else we lose consciousness and quickly die. I suspect that in much the same way, our minds need a constant stream of information. In the absence of enough information, we have a tendency to make things up to fill in the gap. And we usually dig out old memories to accomplish this. If I don't know where my husband is, I will decide that he must be seeing someone else. If my friend is not telling me how she is feeling, I may assume that she is mad at me and is withdrawing in disapproval. It is the mental equivalent of sensory deprivation. When we withhold information from ourselves, or are withheld from, we go crazy, and see things that are not necessarily there.

Blame and Burden

Being responsible is a natural condition that we have to be trained out of. Reclaiming this innate ability can often take a lot of practice. If we take less than 100 percent of the responsibility for our experience, we organize our lives around blame: if I am not completely responsible, then someone else must make up the difference. If we notice ourselves doing this, we know we are not yet at 100 percent responsibility. In couple's therapy I watch this dance of blaming frequently. Each partner maneuvers to get the other one to take responsibility. A common strategy is to take some responsibility, say 30 percent, and then expect our partner to take the other 70 percent ("Well, I know I was late, but you didn't have to get so bent out of shape about it"). If we take 100 percent, we don't require anything from anyone else. They are free to have their own experience. The other result we get at the 100 percent level is that we get our power back. As long as someone else is responsible for our experience (either partly or wholly), then they have the power in the relationship. They have the power to make us feel good or bad. They own a piece of us. And we have to control them in order to get our needs met.

If we take more than 100 percent responsibility for our experience, then we take on a burden. If we are responsible for other people's feelings as well as our own, then we are carrying them on our backs—and the load is heavy. If we feel burdened, we know that we are not at 100 percent. If I am in an interaction with you, and you begin to feel sad, and I decide I am responsible for your sadness, then I own a piece of you. I had then better watch what I do and say so that I can take care of you. I had better watch what you do and say as well, so that I keep you happy. I know what's best.

I often see people attempting to take responsibility, and going overboard into burden with it. I call this the New Age Mistake. It was illustrated by one of my students recently. She had been sexually abused as a child, and when we were talking about the Owning phase she asked this question: "I know that somehow I created this abuse so that I could learn something. But I can't get what that is. What am I not taking responsibility for here?"

I asked her how she felt when she assumed responsibility for her childhood abuse. She replied that she felt heavy and dull. I asked her to play with a change in focus. I asked her to drop taking responsibility for the abuse and start taking responsibility for the heavy dull feeling. This way she could empower herself in the present moment, taking care of her current feelings, and not burden herself with a wrong done to her.

What she then woke up to was another result of her childhood abuse: she had gotten responsibility muddled up. She was able to report that she had this difficulty in her current life, noticing that she would assume responsibility for all kinds of events, working from the New Age assumption that we create our reality. She was using it as a way to reinforce her depression and guilt. She began a practice of postponing her assumption that she was responsible for things around her, and just stuck to being responsible for her direct experience. Over the next year, she was able to recover a tremendous amount of physical energy, particularly sexual.

This getting responsibility muddled into a stew of blame and burden is a common feature of addiction. It takes a lot of our energy to figure out how much responsibility to take, how much others should take, and what we are going to do when others don't agree with our assessments. It all boils down to a core assumption that taking responsibility means admitting wrongness. When we seek abstinence from this addictive assumption, we can recover our ability to respond through direct experience.

Curiously, both blame and burden require us to be the victim, and there is nothing more addictive on this planet than the victim position. I would venture to guess that victimhood takes more lives than any addictive substance, simply because many people would rather die than give up this position. It works because it operates on the assumption that we are *right*. Being right is perhaps even more addictive than being a victim.

Being responsible does not mean that a perpetrator goes free. The perpetrator is 100 percent responsible as well. What we are responsible for when we have been perpetrated against is not succumbing to the victim position, not giving up our power. The Owning phase is about getting our power back. Our empowerment is about using everything that arises in our direct experience as a source of fuel for transformation. Whatever experience we throw away becomes garbage. Whatever experience we use creates fertilizer for our growth.

It is helpful to get a body reading for how blame and burden feel. When I get in a blaming mode I have an almost uncontrollable urge to frown and point my finger. When I feel burdened, I always lose energy and sink down in my chest. By being familiar with these body cues, even when their presence is subtle, I can work with this reactiveness and undo the past that is driving them.

Integrity and responsibility form an alchemical brew. They change the lead of holding back in life to the gold of dancing with it. Most important, they put our bodies back on the track of organismic self-regulation. When we can listen to and trust body messages about what is toxic and what is nourishing, we are able to celebrate life. We have a choice, and the empowerment that this creates is the fuel for continuing the journey of recovery and transformation.

The Critic in the Closet

When the opportunity arises for response, for engagement with life, it flushes out any unresolved wounding or restricting limitations we may have. The opportunity point is like a door opening, and when the door opens, the repressed monster of self-hatred can make a break for it. When we have been taught to limit our awareness and our aliveness, and when we have continued this practice through addiction or habituation, we generate an inner figure I call "the Critic" in order to keep the limitation in place. The Critic uses control, praise, and blame to keep us attending more to our habits than to our direct experience. The Critic often imitates the voice, the gestures, or the body stance of all the people in our history who have criticized us or needed us to be different than we are.

The Critic comes in many shapes and sizes, some of

them quite clever and fetching. One of my favorite critics lives in one of my clients, who describes her as an imperious, well-dressed woman who sits in a big director's chair. She has a very sensible voice and argues very convincingly that my client will never be good enough, will never do it right. Another client characterizes her critic as a Jewish grandmother who, no matter what happens, tells her that it's all right, she's better than all those stupid people anyway.

The Critic is an inherited ancestor, a spirit possession. The Critic is an ally of cognitive addiction, designed to keep direct experience at bay. Direct experience is threatening to it, because the Critic rightly assumes that direct experience would reestablish wholeness and that would put him or her out of a job. What makes the Critic toxic is that we assume she is doing us a favor, keeping us from making even bigger mistakes, somehow acting in our interest. I have had many clients tell me that they needed their Critic because he keeps them from messing up—and this may have been true originally. We may have had to disown parts of ourselves in order to look like what someone else wanted us to look like. And the Critic is the mechanism for keeping parts of ourselves pushed away to a distance where we can disidentify with them enough to feel safe.

The Owning phase work begins when we identify the critical voice and understand its purpose, which is to keep us re-creating our childhood environment. In the service of this status quo, the Critic will often say things that are technically accurate, but that are in fact designed to fragment. The Critic is sneaky—it sounds so real, so convincing. My Critic used to point out ruthlessly whenever I was withholding something or not telling the complete truth. It took me some time to realize that instead of a moment where I could atone for my sins and resolve to do better, this moment was about telling the truth about my critical voice and how it runs me.

The way to work with our Critic is to appreciate him or her. They all came into being for a good reason, and by consciously letting them strut their stuff, we can uncover that primal motivation. I have an inner Critic I call the Good Teacher. This character puffs up my chest, moves my arm in imperious gestures, and has a very deliberate, measured voice. Naturally, she comes out when I teach. She is the part of myself that assumes I must be smart, articulate, erudite, and charming, or the students won't like me. She holds the core belief that deep inside I am really dumb, foolish, and an impostor, and that I need to hide this from my students. She also assumes that I need the approval of my students or I won't be happy or successful.

I began to identify and work with her by "doing" her full out. I would even exaggerate her posture and gestures and attempt to say the smartest, most imperious things I could think of. When I did this, I discovered a whole other side to her; she also really believed that I was the most brilliant, wise, above-it-all teacher in the whole Rocky Mountain region. She craftily created a secret puffed-up Christine that, naturally, I was too polite to reveal. It was when I found both sides of this character that I began to have fun with her rather than let her run me. I will now interrupt a lecture whenever I feel her coming on, and "do" her for my students. It keeps us all laughing, and performs the added function of using me as an apt illustration of inner characters and how to befriend them.

By befriending our characters, we own up to them. We recover our direct experience and access any unfinished wounding that laid them into our bodies, behavior, and thoughts. And we recover our energy, our choosing power, our power to be whole.

The Creative Response

When we vote for being ourselves, for locating ourselves in the present moment, our creativity awakens. Artists and philosophers often envision creativity as the willingness to let an old form and an old way of looking at things dissolve and to allow a new kind of perception and action to occur. Einstein went through this process when he became the first person willing to suspend his belief in the absolute truth of Newtonian physics long enough to envision the theory of relativity. The act of owning our whole selves, of being willing to lay claim to any sensation, emotion, and direct experience, gives birth to our creative potential. We could say, then, that addiction and creativity are opposites; they do not live happily together. Addiction protects us from finding a creative response to our lives, and commiting to a creative life minimizes destructive habits.

Responding creatively to each emerging event in our life occurs through owning ourselves within it. When we own our experience, we access everything we need to get ourselves through the experience in a satisfying way; we access the power for our uniquely creative journey toward communion with essence. We learn to re-create instead of vegetate. Learning to experience and express the truth is so crucial in this endeavor that it is worthy of its own form of attention, its own practices. Below is an exercise designed to help with recovering the truth in our lives.

A Progressive Exercise for Telling the Truth

1. Start with describing your current experience: body sensations, pains, tensions, feelings, thoughts. Be specific, thorough, and descriptive.

2. Stay with these sensations and let them have their full expression. This may necessitate breathing more deeply, moving around, making sounds, or expressing feelings. Let your body guide you to a precise and accurate expression of what you are experiencing. It is important not to make the feeling any different than exactly what it is. We are often trained to make feelings bigger or smaller or different than they really are. If you notice that you are doing this, then make an effort to discover and describe accurately and thoroughly how you are controlling the feeling.

3. Find the underlying statement or position that drives and creates your current experience. If you stay with the above process, this will happen naturally. It can look something like this: The process begins with a question to your spouse, "Why did you do that?" It can then shift to "I was angry when you did that," to "My hands are clenched as I talk to you, and I realize I am furious right now," to "When I go ahead and clench my fists I hear a voice in my head saying 'men will always hurt you,' " to "My mother always said that, and I feel this immense grief that I believed her," to "I realize I am trying to push you away because I assume you will hurt me." We can frequently trace our conflicts back to these kinds of messages that are inherited from our progenitors' unfinished wounding. The messages can be transmitted through what is said, through what is not said, through physical interactions and experiences, through intrauterine "cooking" in

our parents' unfinished feelings, or through emotional control in our early years.

4. Ride the energy that arises from telling successively deeper layers of truth. In the above example, the person might go into deep crying or expressive movement or sound to help her actually finish the commitment she made to her mother to carry on this belief.

5. Stay with the description, feeling, and expressing cycle until you feel completely alive and present. This is the sign that you have found your essential being and are operating from that place.

6. Go out and use this energy for your own nourishment and the nourishment of others. Maybe a bath or a slow walk would feel good. Perhaps you will want to call an old friend and share your experience. It is common to feel so good from this process that we get the urge to finish up all other lingering withheld truths too. Go for it!

One of the most frightening and liberating things I have ever done is to make a commitment to tell the truth in all circumstances, unconditionally, no matter what. It was very similar to my experience of commiting to eating the cookie only if I could stay awake for the experience: I found that it was horribly difficult, excruciatingly provoking. I had no idea how many times in each day I lied. As I explored myself in this squirmingly anguished realization, I found that telling the truth was much more complex than I had previously thought. The big kicker was, as I explained previously, that it was hard for me to distinguish what the truth was. It took me a long time to uncover its nature—that it was an unconditional expression of unarguable direct experience. When I finally had a working sense of what the truth was, I began to explore how it worked in the world.

First, it plainly meant not telling lies. This was hard enough in itself, though it seems quite obvious. I found I had myriad excuses for lying. Some of them looked like this:

- "It's just a little white lie. It won't hurt anyone."
- "If I lie, I'll get the result I want rather than the one I think I'm going to get."
- "If I tell the truth, the other person couldn't handle it. I have to protect them. They would fall apart if they knew."
- "The lie is infinitely more interesting than the truth. I can be so much more entertaining, likeable, etc., if I shape the situation according to what would be fun or dramatic more than what is true."
- "If I tell the truth, I will be disapproved of, found out, abandoned."

With all these seemingly convincing injunctions at my disposal, I wondered if I could ever even clean up this very basic act. When I began to practice this commitment to the truth, working on making it more important than the injunctions to lie, I found that telling the truth got me all excited. The psychologist Fritz Perls once said that fear is excitement without the breath, and when I began to refrain from lying I definitely rode the razor edge of fear and excitement. Remembering to breathe helped immensely. And I found out that I was actually more afraid of this excitement than I was of being disapproved of, thought boring, or criticized.

Next, I unearthed another quality of the truth: it also required that I not withhold. This quality is acknowledged when we swear on a witness stand to tell not only the truth, but the whole truth, and nothing but the truth. The Catholic Church affirms the same principle when it recognizes sins of omission as well as sins of commission. So now I put myself on an even hotter seat. Not only did I have to tell the truth, I had to commit to not concealing the truth. Harriet Lerner examines this idea very eloquently in her book *The Dance of Deception*. In it she examines the effect on a family of the withholding of an innocent but slightly embarrassing truth. The mother decides to tell one daughter but not the other. Even though the information is no big deal, the mother unwittingly creates a family dynamic where one daughter is left out and one in. One is empowered, one is not. The disempowered one mysteriously begins acting out, reaffirming the mother's notion that she cannot handle being told certain things. It was not until the mother was able to undo her withholding that the dysfunctional family dynamic broke.

Once I got clear that telling the truth included not withholding, I began to examine what I was revealing. And here I found the next attribute of the truth: that I could lie in the midst of telling technical truths. I discovered this one day when I caught myself in the act of gossiping. I was talking about one girlfriend to another, and I noticed that somehow I was feeling vaguely off, subtly out of whack. It felt the same sticky way it usually felt when I lied, but I wasn't saying anything that wasn't true. I wasn't even saying anything that was terribly confidential. But what I came to realize was that I was robbing the absent friend of the opportunity to say these things herself, and I was setting my other friend up to know something about her that she wasn't aware of. I had created a dynamic among the three of us that cast me as the informer, the thief of information, and the other two as the receiver of stolen goods and the victim of the crime.

What was I really trying to do here? When I checked in with myself, I realized that what I *truly* wanted at that moment was a feeling of intimacy with my girlfriend. I wanted to be close to her, and I thought I could do that by giving her a choice tidbit of information. The lesson then became one of telling the deeper truth, turning to my girlfriend and telling her how much I cared for her and enjoyed being with her. This opting for directness over indirectness heralded a new level of excitement, one that I'm still learning to handle.

We see another, deeper aspect of the truth when we look at the lives of people who have been willing to put their lives on the line for it. Mahatma Gandhi and Martin Luther King, Jr., are examples of the many people who have been willing to tell the truth of oppression in the face of insurmountable odds. And just like Jesus predicted, the truth set their people free. It was said that the first casualty of the Nazis rule was the truth. Certainly oppression requires lies to be institutionalized. And the truth is the most powerful agent of change in the face of oppression. I am reminded of the awesome power of the repressive military regime that governed Chile in the 1970s. Anyone who criticized it, or who exercised any free speech, was dragged away and never released. Thousands of Chileans suffered this fate, and the regime showed no signs of letting up. What began to happen quite spontaneously was that women—the mothers and wives and sisters of the missing—gathered in the town squares. They would bring pictures of their lost loved ones and show them to each other and to passersby. Some began to show the pictures to passing cars, with the simple word written below the photo:

Disappeared. They came to be called *los desaparecidos*—
the Disappeared—and these brave women, who were willing to simply sit and tell the unarguable truth, were credited with being one of the major forces of conscience that
eventually brought down the regime. We can all be agents
of this kind of change in our daily lives: by committing to
the truth as an unconditional practice, we liberate ourselves and all others with whom we come in contact.

Taking ownership of our lives can have tremendous effects in the world. This truth was never more eloquently
put than by Nelson Mandela, a political prisoner for almost three decades, who rose to become president of
South Africa. Here is a fragment of his 1994 presidential
inauguration speech:

> Our deepest fear is not that we are inadequate. Our deepest
> fear is that we are powerful beyond measure. It is our light,
> not our darkness, that most frightens us. We ask ourselves,
> who am I to be brilliant, gorgeous, talented, and fabulous?
> Actually, who are you not to be? You are a child of God.
> Your playing small doesn't serve the world. There's noth-
> ing enlightening about shrinking so that other people
> won't feel insecure around you. We were born to make
> manifest the glory of God that is within us. It's not just in
> some of us, it's in everyone. As we let our own light shine,
> we unconsciously give others permission to do the same.
> As we are liberated from our own fear, our presence auto-
> matically liberates others.

Deeply owning the truth in its deepest manifestations
can be transformational. It can be much more creative energy, much more excitement (and breath!), and most important, it can make it so that we don't have to hide any-
more. We become transparent to life, able to dissolve

defenses against the old beliefs that we used to conceal. We can learn to take responsibility for being visible in relationships instead of demanding that others see us while we remain partially hidden. In the Owning phase we practice making what we are aware of visible. Below are further exercises designed to increase this visibility.

Exercises for the Owning Phase

1. Choose an historical event that troubles you. Imagine it in your mind as vividly as possible. Note what sensations and actions occur in your body as you do this. Does your chest flutter? Does your stomach get tight? Attend to these sensations and feelings and allow them to occur by breathing into them and making any movements that express them. Stay with this process until the movement feels satisfying and complete. Note when these same sensations may occur in your daily life and work with doing this exercise when they occur.

2. Feel the boundaries of your body, both by touching them yourself and by sensing them while touching objects and other people. How does that feel? What do you remember being told about your body's boundaries? Are certain boundary areas more OK than others? Is there any relationship between how you experience your body's boundaries and tendencies you have to keep yourself isolated or fused with others? It may be helpful to draw pictures of yourself (don't worry about style and technique) and look at how you have drawn your boundaries.

3. Identify someone or something that you blame for something you are currently experiencing. Now let yourself really get into it. Go ahead and pretend that you can

say anything you feel about this person. Let your body go for it, assuming postures, words, and gestures that go along with the blame. How does your body feel as you are doing this? Note the location and intensity of your sensations. Now forget the object of blame and focus on the sensations and feelings. Do they feel familiar? Do they remind you of anyone? Often we discover that we have been on the receiving end of tirades just like this one—and it is hard for us to admit that we are now playing the part of the very person who oppressed us. Allow yourself to feel your feelings and tell the truth about being both the victim and the abuser in this scenario. Repeat the exercise using someone else or something else you feel burdened by.

4. Find something you hate about yourself. Spend some time getting a feel for this part of yourself—do any images come to mind? Do any sensations come up in your body? And note this: the hated part of yourself has many attributes. Push aside the negative aspects and name some of the positive ones. For instance, you may hate the part of yourself that got out of control and yelled at your boss this week. If you look deeply, you might also see that this is also the part of you that doesn't hesitate to stand up for yourself. Our hated parts usually contain some important life skills, or else they wouldn't stick around. Take some time to appreciate the qualities that work for you in this part of yourself. Breathe into it, and notice what occurs in your body. Appreciate any body states that may arise.

5. The next time you catch yourself in self-criticism, let yourself play with it. Give the Critic a voice, a body posture, a significant gesture. Find what movements and looks the Critic would use. Now really go for it and let the Critic loose. The more you exaggerate the Critic, the more absurd he or she becomes and the more you can play. And

by identifying the behavioral strategies of the Critic, you can be more alert to his or her presence next time. The next time, greet your Critic. Say hi to him. Befriend her and also challenge her.

7

Recovery in Relationships
The Body Dancing

*Addiction destroys love as well as freedom. A lover
is willing to be moved. The addict clings to the
status quo.* —SAM KEEN, *The Passionate Life*

The next phase of the Moving Cycle is that of Acceptance,
the bedrock of love and of relationships. The dictionary
defines *acceptance* as "an act of believing in, or receiving
willingly." Acceptance grows out of the consistent practice
of telling the truth and taking responsibility. What occurs
when we do this is that we begin to form an unconditional
relationship to ourselves. When we don't withdraw from
truth, we accept it for what it is. We don't put conditions
on our experience: "This feeling is OK, but this one isn't."
"This thought is acceptable; this one isn't." When we relate in an unconditional way to our experience, we become
accepting of it. And we can enjoy an open attitude toward
it. I believe this is what in AA is called serenity.

When I accept my experience I can tolerate its intensity;
I can learn from it. I can even find joy in it. In fact, I become nourished and joyful at the *process* of acceptance,
more than at its actual content. It actually feels good,
whether my acceptance is of the pain in my toe or of the
beauty in my lover's face. It is the act of being with my

experience that is satisfying, not the content of what is happening. This is a crucial distinction for people in addictive processes. When we are addicted, we see that thing, that substance or behavior, as our gratifier. When it is not present, we feel longing and anxious craving. Our experience is conditional on that thing being present. When we drop our addiction, we get gratification from the very process of experiencing in itself. Since experience is always there, we can receive unlimited gratification from simply participating with it. It is an unlimited source.

When I accept myself, love is reborn. When nothing will make me abandon myself or hurt myself, love is present—I am loving myself in the same unconditional way that a parent can love a child. If I did not get this unconditional love the first time around, I must discover and re-create it in myself. I believe that a useful definition of love is "unconditional acceptance."

Most of us have learned to view acceptance with suspicion and mistrust. We equate acceptance with acquiescence, or with the condoning of indiscriminate behavior. This occurs when we get confused about what acceptance is. Acceptance is not something we can give to a person or thing. It only exists as a function of our relationship to our own experience. In other words, I cannot accept you; what I do is to accept unconditionally all the feelings I have when I am with you, all the thoughts I have about you. This means that I own that they are mine and are not created by you. It also means that I am committed to participating with these feelings. I accept my own experience. I am not here to validate or invalidate yours. When I accept my experience, I commit one of the most loving acts possible—I stay out of the way of your experience.

One of the most hurtful things we can do in relation-

ships is to believe that the other person caused us to feel
the way we are feeling: "You made me angry!" as if there
was a button they pushed that we, like motorized toys,
had no choice but to obey. Psychologists have a fancy
phrase for this: the external locus of control. We actually
believe that others are in control of us, that they determine
our feelings and experiences. This externalizing of control
is fundamental to any addiction. We believe that the alcohol, the food, the cigarettes, the obsessive thinking, are
what is in control, not us. This putting someone or something else in control occurs when we do not accept our
own experience. If we decide our current experience is not
right, then we have a tendency to attribute this not right-
ness to an external source.

When I wake up to, take ownership of, and accept my
current experience, I internalize my locus of control. I am,
as Ernie Larsen puts it, driving my own bus. When I do
this, I am giving others a lot of space to be themselves. In
a sense, it is an act of celebrating them, but that acceptance
is only a by-product of my own self-acceptance. It is in
the context of this space that we create for others to be
themselves that relationships can form. We can see people
accurately, without any filters of what we would like them
to be or think is best for them. We have plenty of space to
get close and to get separate.

When we accept our experience, we find an internal
locus through which we generate our own self-boundary.
And when we have a boundary, contact becomes possible.
Contact is the food and fuel of relationship. Fritz Perls said
that contact is an essential human need and that all other
human needs are met when we can self-regulate our contact functions. It is at this self-boundary that addictions
are generated and released. Acceptance of what I am cur-

rently experiencing creates a self-boundary, inside of which is my creative core. This creative center is inherently lovable because there are no conditions to it. By reclaiming this creative center, I become capable of creative contact with others. And in the space of that contact, love for others is born.

Commitment is an essential feature of the Acceptance phase. By committing unconditionally to our own experience, we set the stage for our ability to commit to relationship. Before my own recovery was in place, I had a consistent habit of leaving relationships because they got too intense (whether intensely awful *or* intensely wonderful). I could only make conditional commitments to others. If I had a few experiences in the relationship that I didn't like, I would leave, on the assumption that it was the relationship that was causing the negative experiences. When I stopped externalizing the unpleasant experiences, I found that it was much easier to stay in a relationship.

When I get in trouble in relationships, I now know to ask myself the million-dollar question: What am I committed to right now? If the answer turns out to be that I am committed to being right, to being a victim, or to getting my way, then I know I am somehow not accepting my current experience. And I can then make a conscious effort to wake up and to own my experience.

When we are committed to ourselves and to a relationship, we can create dialogue, which is a kind of exchange of nourishment with the other. When we commit to anything other than ourselves and relationship, we create monologue and travelogue. In monologue we indulge in the desire to hear ourselves talk. No one else need be involved, unless for propriety's sake. We get to see things our way. Travelogue is making the story, the event, the upset, more important than the relationship. We move down a well-worn path, ending up at the same old place.

Dialoguing is an exciting event, and most of us have to learn to tolerate it and to enjoy its intensity. Dialogue obeys the law of physics that when two objects get close to each other they generate heat. Part of our divine life lesson is to learn to bask in the glow of this heat created by relationship without getting burned. In order to do this we constantly negotiate how close and how separate we need to be to find just the right amount of heat that will warm us—any further out and we will be cold and too distant, any closer in and we will enmesh with the other, lose our boundaries, and get burned. It is a deliciously changeable dance born through waking up and owning our experience.

Dialoguing involves paying conscious attention to the heat of relationship. As I get closer to my partner, I increase my need to tell the truth and to feel and express my feelings. This creates a bond that holds me and my partner safe through the surges of energy that wash up on the shore of every relationship. In dialoguing, we attend not only to ourselves but also to our partner and to the energy that we create together. Often we keep ourselves unaware of the energy, and when this happens it can overwhelm us.

I'm reminded of one of the most pleasurable and exciting things I ever did as a teenager—to swim in the surf near my home in southern California. The exhilaration of jumping up to cut through a swell, of diving under the big ones, of riding them just as they crested, was truly a teenage epiphany. Once, after a big storm, I ran directly into the water to play, not taking the time to study the swells and how they were breaking. By the time I realized that some monster waves were coming in sets every five minutes, I was in too deep to get out. Each surge of water landed on me, bashed the air out of my lungs, and tossed me like a rag. Just as I was losing consciousness, a lifeguard saved me.

Relationships carry some of the biggest waves I have ever seen. And if we don't respect and stay awake to that, we can drown in them. Dialoguing keeps me safe in the water, keeps me swimming with the relationship rather that being tossed about by it. If I had taken a few minutes to study both myself and the water, I could have seen the depth that was safe and fun for that day—the depth that maximized my joy, that enabled me to play very fully. Like waves on a shoreline, relationships change levels constantly. So, I stay awake, I oscillate my attention, and I commit to feeling and expressing my experience unconditionally, and only then, I step into the water.

Dialoguing recovers our ability to recognize essence in others. It helps us constantly to negotiate contact at the boundaries, penetrating and absorbing in an oscillatory manner. If we don't access the essence, the beauty, in others we cut ourselves off from letting beauty bathe and penetrate us. And from that point, our own beauty cannot long stand. Affirming the beauty of the world is a biological imperative, and occurs through the mechanism of relationship.

Breaking Our Hearts

I once heard a beautiful teaching story: A rabbi told his students that here in this school they would lay the teachings on their hearts. One child raised her hand and asked, "But Rabbi, why don't you put the teachings *in* our hearts?"

"Oh, no," the Rabbi answered, "only God can do that. Here we put the teaching *on* our hearts so that when they break, the teachings will fall in."

Love breaks our hearts, and it is good that it does so. The Acceptance phase is designed to crack open the walls of our heart so that it can grow to contain even more love. Whenever we fail to take the opportunities that love gives us, our hearts shatter. When we stay in dialogue with life our hearts break open and more aliveness flows in, increasing our capacity for love. Instead of feeling love through a broken, shattered heart, we can shed our old heart boundaries like a snake sheds its skin in order to grow. Love requires that we transmute in this way. If we resist its call, the cracking open will be a wounding. Even this wounding can be transformed into a wake-up call, an imperative to make more room for love.

One of the first things I do when I begin working with a couple is ask them to stand facing each other and to play with getting closer to and farther away from each other. When one partner gets farther away, does the other feel abandoned? When he or she gets closer, does the other one feel smothered? Who initiates contact? Who initiates separation? Do one or both make the other person responsible for the feelings they are having? What kinds of stories do they make up about their partner's behavior? A surprisingly complete diagnosis can be made through observing this simple behavior.

The Acceptance phase occurs after Awareness and Owning. When these two phases are established, whether it be in an individual or between partners, the business of acceptance is revealed. When I have thoroughly ridden the waves of energy generated by awakeness and responsiveness, I am changed literally on a cellular level. I have been moved by life into a more perfect union with myself and with others. What acceptance requires is that I deeply acknowledge this, and be willing to hang out with the new me. It is like being at a birth; I cradle the newly arrived being and I deeply greet it, welcome it, and bathe it in my love.

I witness the Acceptance phase in my clients every time one has a felt level experience of being themselves in the here and now. Feeling this moment in this place, and feeling separate from the momentum of personal history, cracks open their self-concept and makes room for so much more. I become more than my concepts of myself— more than my body, more than my feelings, more than my thoughts. There is space for all these to occur, and more. It is the space itself that is me.

Acceptance creates space. Space allows room for the personal transformation that life constantly requires of us. By riding our direct experience into the Acceptance phase, we create the space to hold our experiences. It is in this phase that our spiritual natures can be recovered. How we articulate this space is up to us, but accessing it comes through accepting unconditionally both what is and how "what is" is going to change.

I work with a suicidal client who had such a difficult childhood that he described each day of it as "climbing up a sheer cliff face in the dark." It took us over a year to establish an Awareness phase, and another for him to consistently own his experience. As we entered the third year, he began to confront the lack of love that his worldview had created. He finally realized that this lack of love was an important (if indirect) act of revenge against his mother for warping him so badly. We are working now on creating space in his life for relationships through reclaiming the ability to ride the waves of his hateful feelings toward his mother in a direct manner, realizing that to do so will not kill him—and neither will he then have to project these feelings onto others.

Acceptance is first and foremost a body-centered process. It starts with an acknowledgement of physical feeling and proceeds to loving ourselves for having this feeling. We can reclaim self-acceptance by practicing on the most basic level of reality, our body.

Below are some exercises designed to reclaim our natural ability for acceptance. They work with the basic components of acceptance: the ability to regulate contact and enjoy the heat of it.

Exercises for the Acceptance Phase

1. When an intense feeling arises, practice breathing fully so that your body can form a container for the experience. Let your body move around or make sounds with this energy so that it can generate enough space to express the feeling accurately. Keep breathing and moving until the feeling is complete. This is an exercise in tolerating and even welcoming the energy of a feeling within yourself, without projecting it out onto others.

2. Recall someone for whom you feel great love. Be aware of how that love feels in your body. Now breathe fully as you send this same quality of love toward some part of yourself that you have hated. Treat that part of yourself like a small child that needs to be held in safety and love.

3. Find a partner and stand facing each other. Slowly walk toward him or her and then away, sensing the point at which the distance feels too far or too near. First, you

do the approaching and parting while your partner stays still. Next, have your partner approach you and move away. Then do it simultaneously. What feelings and sensations arise? Is it harder to get close? Do you feel panicky when you get separate? What about when your partner is doing the moving? Is it OK to let him or her go? Is it irritating when he or she gets too close? Acknowledge and breathe into the sensations that arise. Find the right distance for right now and talk about this exercise with your partner. How does this remind you of other relationships you have had?

4. Recall someone for whom you feel some disapproval. Spend a moment to identify and get clear on the nature of your disapproval. Now get curious about what feelings lie underneath those opinions. Do you feel angry? Hurt? This is your experience. Open up to it. Stay curious as you explore what sensations arise in your body; feel the texture of the emotions and the thoughts. Do they feel in any way familiar? Have you felt them before? When was the first time you ever remember feeling these feelings? Whom were they toward? Ask yourself if there is anything that is incomplete about that old event or any subsequent similar events. Follow the procedure for dealing with an intense feeling to help complete this.

5. Sit down facing a loved one. State to your partner what you are aware of in yourself at that moment, starting with your body. Then have your partner do the same. Progress to alternating between being aware of what is going on in you and what you notice about the other person. Remember to stay descriptive—only describe things that are unarguable, like body sensations or feelings. Sooner or later, this exchange will generate some heat. You or your partner may feel excited, embarrassed, or irritated.

Tell your partner about this, then increase your breathing and moving to make a space in which this level of intimacy can occur. Keep telling the truth and breathing and moving through the heat until you feel that you have increased your usual level of sharing in a satisfying way.

6. Recall a time when you felt heartbroken. Play with reframing this event in your mind. Imagine that love was asking you to make your heart bigger as a result of this encounter. What do you need to acknowledge and accept within yourself or toward another person to make this so?

7. Sit yourself down and turn your attention inside. Do a body check-in, from head to toe. Then begin to contemplate a problem you are currently experiencing. Envision the problem as having shape and size. Let it fill your vision. Now imagine that you could step back from it, seeing not only the problem but the space around it. Notice the space itself. Stay with this contemplation of space for a while. When you feel finished, check into your body again. And ask yourself, "How can I create some space around this problem in my daily life?"

8

What Do I Practice?

When we don't get our early needs met, not only can we become addicted to need substitutes, but we also can have trouble knowing what we want, how we feel, and where our limits are. We have seen in the previous chapters how we can regain these lost capacities again through the power of telling the truth and accepting our current experience. When we tell the truth about our experience, we access our authentic self, our essence. We also liberate the tremendous wellspring of life energy that is stored there. This energy works best when it gets used. This chapter is about completing our recovery through the Action phase of the Moving Cycle. True to the axiom "Use it or lose it," recovery and transformation require regular practice. When we practice our recovery in the world, we reaffirm and reinforce it, creating space for even more transformation to occur.

By accepting our own experience, we cease projecting our disowned material onto the world, and the world can exist for us in a clear and real way. Instead of being a reflection of our unfinished wounding, it is simply there in all its commonplace beauty. When we cease requiring it to feed our unmet needs and simply relate to it as it is, a nourishing and pleasurable exchange can result.

My friend Gay Hendricks put it succinctly when he

stated that healing is about becoming a producer in the world more than a consumer. When we are addicted to anything, whether it is a process or a substance, we become a societal consumer. Quite literally, addiction costs this country billions of dollars each year in lost wages, crime, accidents, and injury. Addicts of all kinds are flooding our health-care systems, threatening to crush it. On a less literal level, our addictions sap the energy of our friends and loved ones as well as us. Addiction robs us of our creativity, and without this fundamental problem-solving tool, the world actually does become a harder place to live in for us all.

Recovery involves turning this drain of energy around. Contributing our energy to the world not only feels good and does good, but it is actually a fundamental action of recovery. When we demonstrate our healing and our life-affirming action in the world, we are recovering its beauty and its energy as well. We do not have to become Mother Teresa, or join the Peace Corps—often do-gooding can itself be an addictive process. But contributing our energy to the world is about giving the parts of ourselves that we have recovered, showing them to the world, exercising their muscles, and bringing them into the light.

It is interesting that *what* we recover is always useful. It may be out sense of humor or our sharp wits or our physical stamina or our kindness. It may be our ability to pay the bills or hold a job or be a good parent. These qualities we recover are essential to manifest into the world, both for our sake and for our environment's. They create the world as a place where bills are paid and jokes are told and laughter is heard. We create the world through our actions.

What we have lost to addiction—and therefore what we

recover from it—is individual. When I stopped eating sugar addictively I became more outgoing and more interested in other people. I realized that I had more energy available for relationships, and I began to teach classes on addiction. A friend of mine who gave up cigarettes began choreographing fantastic modern dances. If I have been laid low by a life threatening addiction, for a while recovery is measured by simply staying alive. This is a simple gift, but an immeasurably valuable one. When we keep acting on our recovery, not assuming that it stops at a certain point, we recover not only our lives but also our joy in being alive, and a *higher purpose* for being alive. What is your higher purpose? The higher it gets, the more brilliant a world results.

Our bodies are the model, the template for action. Our whole wiring is built on a loop of nerves receiving input, then producing action upon that input. Our bodies unceasingly echo this structure in the expanding and contracting of the beating heart and in the wavelike breathing of our lungs. With breathing, we take the world in as air, we use parts of it, and we express out what is left, including parts of ourselves. The carbon dioxide gases in our outbreath nourish all the world's green plants, as their exhalation creates our oxygen. This action is a basic life-balancing exchange and is a metaphor for what is reestablished in recovery. We start with our bodies, as they give us the clues as to how to do it.

From birth and even before we have an innate capacity to feel blissful, orgasmic pleasure, simply by being in our bodies. Most of us get trained out of using this capacity to the hilt. Any family or culture or religion that represses pleasure creates addiction as a substitute for it. To recover from addiction we not only must abstain from something but must also recover our natural capacity to feel joy. This is the motivation of life, the basis of any action. To recover the world we must move—we must literally get up off our butts and dance.

The major problem with the Action phase of the Moving Cycle is that we are just not used to feeling good. If we have been battling an addiction, we have gotten used to struggling with shame, self-hatred, and a sense of powerlessness. Our brain, psyche, and body are programmed to register this as the normal state of affairs. What we are used to, we will repeat. Just like any other object in the universe, we are subject to the laws of momentum. Doing something automatically is much easier than doing something that requires conscious action, even if the new action involves confidence rather than shame, self-love rather than self-deprecation. A habit is a habit because it has worked at some time in the past, and it was so successful that our nervous system learned to repeat it. Self-destructive behaviors are often simply our best choice in a bad situation.

How do we reprogram our nervous system to learn new input? How do we operate on a higher level of aliveness, fun, and integrity? The answer is that we can give our nervous system the input to rewire itself by practicing new behaviors. We cannot simply sit and visualize our way through recovery (though that might be a good way to rehearse). We also cannot recover by sitting in our rooms and writing. We cannot recover by going to meetings and simply listening. We must act, for it is only in action that our bodies can physically change their old patterns of behavior. We shape ourselves as individuals and as a species by interacting with our environment. This is an evolutionary imperative that we cannot ignore. Healing and transformation only have meaning when they are set loose in the world.

One action that bears specific attention is the action of witnessing other people—seeing them clearly, as they truly are. As was stated before, humans have an inborn need to be seen, to be observed and absorbed without judgment or repression. From seventeen years of private and public practice, I have come to see that most of us need remedial help in learning how to see others deeply and clearly. We also need help learning to communicate what we see to people in a way that is nourishing and friendly. Just like we inhale and exhale, we both give and receive attention and feedback from others. Our ability to accurately and lovingly reflect others to themselves is a tremendous "producer" behavior, one that can generate immense benefit all around us. When we learn how to give feedback to others, we learn a form of expressing love that makes people glow and blossom.

Giving feedback is a rarely practiced art. Most of us only know how to give criticism or praise (two of the Critic's favorite modes). We disapprove of what someone else is doing, and we let them know that it is their problem, not ours. We feel uncomfortable, scared, or helpless, and we try to get the other person to change so we will feel better. The bottom-line statement is, "If you were different then I could continue to operate the way I am used to, and that would be more comfortable." In other words, we can maintain the stances and positions that keep us addicted and unhappy.

Our style of giving feedback or criticism stems directly from the way we recieved it as children. Often as children we are not encouraged to be who we are but who our parents think we should be. The more dysfunctional the family, the greater the gap is between who we are and who we are "supposed" to be. Who we are supposed to be is usually (1) someone who does not challenge the family setup, and (2) someone who fulfills the unmet needs of the caretakers. Both of these criteria can be transmitted both verbally and nonverbally through the mechanism of criticism and selective praise.

As we grow up, we may internalize this process and pass it on to our children, spouses, and friends. The way out clearly lies along the same path as any addiction recovery, since this, too, is all about unsatisfying substitutes for real, unmet needs. While on this path we can practice changing our habits of criticism to ones of feedback. First, how do we tell the difference between criticism and feedback? Here is a preliminary list of the differences:

FEEDBACK	CRITICISM
Is descriptive	Is interpretive
Is value-neutral	Is judgmental
Has no agenda	Has an agenda
Provides multiple options	Reduces options
Is growth-affirming	Affirms control

Description is a wonderful thing because it provides information we can use. Feedback describes an experience. Hearing that I squeeze my eyes every time I talk about my father is more useful than hearing that I obviously have unfinished stuff with my father. Description gives me reference points to work with, places of inquiry that I can investigate. Our ability to describe what someone else is doing shows them that we see them. Feeling seen by others is one of our most primal needs. Truly reflecting what someone is doing can be like giving them a mirror in which they can see themselves.

Most of us have trouble distinguishing between description and interpretation. Description is verifiable and unarguable. Anyone can see it: "I have a tingly feeling in my stomach." "Gorbachev has a birthmark on his head." "You raised your voice and clenched your teeth when you asked me where I was last night."

Interpretation is an explanation of something. It is the viewer's *opinion* of what he or she has observed. It is already subject to our projections and past history. It imposes our worldview onto someone else's experience: "You're afraid of love." "You're too tired to talk about this now." An interpretation may be accurate, but it is also subject to the viewer's mood, intention, state of arousal, belief systems, and so forth. It reinforces the codependent assumption that someone else knows me better than I do.

Many forms of therapy are interpretive. Their function is to interpret behavior, attributing unconscious motivations to the client's actions. Therapists may interpret dreams in an attempt to explain hidden messages. Though many therapies are brilliant and intuitive, they can fall short in the face of addiction because interpretation, by its very nature, can be toxic for the addict. When I am recovering from an addictive process, I am trying to find my way back from being interpreted and criticized to the point of being able to *describe what is*. Description is an act of creating a boundary that as addicts we so desperately need. The boundary is formed by the bare-bones description of experience.

The second feature of feedback is that it is value-neutral. In other words, it doesn't assign a value of good or bad to what is being described. This concept is quite foreign to most people. I had one anorectic client who absolutely believed that if she didn't constantly criticize her weight, she would blow up like a balloon. It is the criticism that keeps her evil, fat self in check.

As parents, most of us subscribe to the belief that we must instill a sense of right and wrong in our children, or they could turn out to be amoral sociopaths. What this usually translates into is the practice of controlling children's actions so that they will conform, rather than helping them to develop their own sense of judgment about what works and what doesn't work. We make the child's essence right or wrong, as if *right* and *wrong* were some external and arbitrary laws of the universe and as if the child were incapable of learning from his or her own experience.

As addicts we basically think we are wrong. We drink or smoke or practice other self-destructive behaviors because we are trying to anesthetize a poor self-concept. Practicing our wrongness involves desensitizing ourselves to our body so that it cannot give us feedback about what works and what doesn't. When we don't have our body as a reference point, we look outside of ourselves for our sense of what is right and what to do about it. We turn to substances, people, or behaviors that prop us up with rules and boundaries. And since they are outside us, we get to mess up in order to sabotage and rebel against those externally imposed rules. The cycle continues. Recovering our bodies helps us to drop our dependency on those external reference points, and to develop a value-neutral ability to sense what is.

Assigning a value to what another person is doing is a good way to become one of their crutches. When you are a crutch you spend all your time and energy holding up both your sense of right and wrong and the person attached to it. Then you get to feel bad when they fall. Sound familiar? We criticize others because we are programmed to think that what we feel is wrong or right, and someone must be blamed for it or burdened with it. It gives us that reassuring and familiar sense of being a victim. We also praise others so that we can control them and their opinion of themselves and us. Praise can be just as destructive as blame, as it still relies on an external reference point.

How do we get from "You are a jerk to talk to me like that" to "I feel scared and small when you say that"? We go back to the place of descriptive truth. We go back to our bodies. Feedback describes our direct experience. It lets someone know what effect he or she has in the world and on me without making them wrong or bad. It is hard for people to hear that they are wrong—it usually just reinforces their original wounding, and they have few choices but to defend themselves as a survival mechanism. Often people will unconsciously try to hurt you so that you *will* get mad at them and make them feel wrong. Only then do they feel familiar to themselves, and familiar equals safe.

This brings us to the next feature of feedback. It has no agenda. How many times have we said, "But I want him to see what he is doing to himself!" Another favorite is, "She needs to understand that what she is doing is wrong." It may be that the person in question is messing up. But if we *need* to explain this to him or her from some agenda of our own, we will again pollute that person's growth opportunity with our own unfinished business. There are a handful of common agendas: to control, to wound, and to deflect excitement.

The agenda of control is familiar to all of us. It is an essential feature of addiction, as it establishes a kind of defensive boundary where none has developed naturally. We feel safe in this boundary of control and feel that if we can just get other people to control themselves too, then all the boundaries will be secure. Within the agenda of control, we give pseudo-feedback like this: "Perhaps if you just realized how horrible you look when you yell like that . . ." or "If you just stopped drinking everyone else around you would feel so much better. You would feel better too." These statements may be in response to a person's messing up, but they are designed to control behavior rather than offer an opportunity to heal. The bottom line is that we want to avoid some painful truth in ourselves when we try to control others—we are avoiding uncomfortable feelings in ourselves, such as helplessness, fear, or rage.

We also control others by giving them the impression that they cause us to have certain experiences, and are therefore responsible for our bad time: "He made me so mad!" or "He hurt my feelings!" People do broadcast their energy to us, but it is our internal processing of this energy that creates our experience. And our internal processing is referented to our own early imprinting. When we are children we are dependent on our family to provide a safe and loving container in which we can grow. If this container was not entirely safe, we will come to our age of independence assuming that we are still not safe and that others are still responsible for our safety. Other people determine our experience. We assume that they are responsible for what we feel. The only way to feel powerful is to control what they do.

Many of us have been raised to believe that only wounding others will produce change. In a limited sense this is true—being hit by a Mack truck will produce change. It may be that others wounded us to force us to change, so we adopt the agenda ourselves. Or the behavior may result from our impulse to lash back at someone we believe has wounded us. In a violent household, hurting someone back can be the only way of getting them to stop hurting *you.* I worked with one client who was going through a divorce. She talked about how she would call up her ex and with razorlike accuracy recount his many faults. She would become enraged when he didn't agree with her and mend his ways. As she explored the tightness in her jaw that arose as she was telling me this, she realized she wanted to hurt him with these words. Staying with her clenched jaw produced a memory of taking beatings from her father while he expounded on what she had done wrong.

The other common agenda in feedback is to deflect excitement. Other people's actions can generate a lot of energy in us. If we don't have much experience with tolerating or enjoying our energy, we may try to deflect it. We will project it onto others ("Now don't get too excited!") or try to get them to stop what they are doing so that we will feel less frightened. If we tell a friend he is unconsciously flirting with us, then we can ignore our own attraction to him, which we may experience as threatening. If we tell a colleague to grow up, we can avoid the parental feelings we have toward her. In any case, by deflecting excitement we avoid the inconvenience of getting stirred up and having to take responsibility for it.

Agendas are deadly to feedback. They split the surface motive of caring from the underlying motive of withdrawal and pain. Genuine feedback is characterized by a lack of attachment to an outcome. Expecting the other person to provide the outcome is not only codependent, but sabotages both our ability to be genuine and hers.

When feedback has nothing of our unfinished wounding attached to it, it can become like the simple completion of a circuit: there is an experience, then there is its expression. What has come into and through us will come out from us. Our bodies understand this circuit phenomenon, as they are constantly engaged in it in other ways. Every experience must be completed, or it is stored in the body and in the mind and will constantly reassert itself in an effort to find completion. Telling the truth is one of the most powerful ways to complete our internal circuits. Giving feedback is one of the best ways to complete the circuit of relationship to others. It can be a gift of information, which our minds constantly need.

Feedback creates more options in a relationship. If I can describe what my partner is doing, then he or she has an opportunity to investigate this behavior without defensiveness. If we are busy defending ourselves from a judgmental assessment that carries an agenda with it, we are not safe to examine our own behavior. Genuine feedback carries with it only verifiably true information. With the truth before us, we can choose to make more contact with the person who is witnessing us, as well as with our own inner being. We can choose to change our actions, to seek help, or to get back to it another time. We feel free to use this information in our own best interests.

Being criticized decreases our options: we can basically only fight or flee or freeze. We can fight directly by being aggressive, or indirectly by being passive or withholding. We can flee by leaving or by tuning ourselves or the other person out. We can freeze by simply trying to be invisible in the relationship. If movement tags are not strong enough to affect the fight, freeze, or flight mechanism in our bodies, we will turn to behaviors and substances.

The last characteristic of feedback is that it is growth-affirming. Real feedback allows us to self-regulate, given the proper information and nourishment. Because it is a description of either what we are doing or what is occurring in others, it addresses that part of ourselves oriented toward growth and fulfillment. If my friend observes that every time I talk about my ex-husband, I stop breathing fully, I can then play with consciously altering that pattern. What happens when I talk about him while breathing fully? What usually happens is that by choosing this new option I get to experience whatever it is that is keeping me from being fully alive.

Criticism only affirms control. It gives us one more experience of being wrong and incapable of being right without the constant criticism of others to keep us in line. It affirms that our boundaries are outside of us and that we would fall down without them. It retards the growth and development of internal limits that form from our experience of what works and what doesn't work.

So how do we distinguish between feedback and criticism, and consistently choose feedback? Below is a list of rules for the road.

Guidelines for Giving Feedback

Only give feedback when it is asked for. It is crucial to give feedback only when there is an opening to receive it. Only the receiver knows when this is. It is also the receiver's decision as to whether he or she is safe and the situation is safe enough to warrant being receptive to new informa-

tion. You can ask if the person is interested in your feedback about what just happened. You can let others know
when you feel receptive to feedback. These limits need to
be respected in order to maintain a safe growth environment. I have a deal with my best friend that she can give
me feedback anytime she wants. This kind of carte blanche
for feedback is a feature of a very special relationship.

Don't give feedback unless you can stay descriptive. If
you are feeling upset in a situation, take care of yourself
first. Tell the truth about it. Feel you feelings. Only when
you have done this clearing and completing of your own
circuits are you capable of giving feedback to someone
else. I have sometimes handled this kind of situation suc-
cessfully by saying something like, "I'm feeling so upset
about myself that I can't give you feedback yet, but I can
say that when you were talking I noticed that your brow
was furrowed, and I remember you doing that before
when a similar thing happened." Only say what you can
describe accurately and thoroughly. What you can describe is what you experience with your five senses, and
what feelings you experience within your own being with
those same senses.

Look for the pattern. Feedback is useful when it gives
people information about how they are restricting or en-
hancing their aliveness. We restrict our aliveness through
patterned responses to fresh situations. Movement tags are
a type of pattern. Another pattern is the repetition of the
same response over and over to a similar situation—
always falling in love with people who are emotionally
withdrawn, for example. Or always drinking at night after
the children are in bed. The behavior can be very subtle,
like my own tendency to breathe shallowly when I talk
about politics. Illuminating the pattern where and when

it arises is crucial to recovery and can be tremendously powerful.

Find an anchor in the body. Since our body is the part of ourselves that is the most observable, it is often the easiest place to start. And finding out how the body is tagging a behavior gives the receiver a very clear option for experimentation. The body can be used to wake up to the underlying withdrawal from aliveness. Tell the person what their body does when they talk about a certain subject or when they describe how they feel. It gives them a direct experience of being seen as well as a reference point from which to grow.

Affirm the beauty. Feedback is the completion of a loop of witnessing. Feedback helps us to form limits, but it also helps us to expand and bloom. Hearing affirmations of our innate beauty and grace sets the stage for flowering. The best affirming kind of feedback is also descriptive. We rightly mistrust blanket praise, as it often has an ulterior motive. Practice giving descriptive feedback about beauty. I have heard this called "the attitude of gratitude." I used to have such a block about this that I had to start by practicing on landscapes and sunsets before I got good enough at it to reflect human beauty and grace. It is often quite exciting and threatening to practice affirming beauty—we come dangerously close to bliss and other associated peak experiences.

Feedback is one of the greatest gifts we can give each other. It holds within it the power of the unconditional witness. It is an affirmation that I see you and I am with you and I value you enough to reflect back to you what you are doing. It maintains and increases the possibility of contact and intimacy. It breaks the back of the addictive process.

The Action phase fulfills our biological imperative to reproduce; what we are reproducing is adaption and change and the whole species can benefit. It is a practicing of what we have become. Scientists who study the brain remark on how much the brain runs on constants, and how it is the laying down of constants that gives us our biological momentum. This is true throughout the body as well. The previous phases of the Moving Cycle have been about dissolving the momentum of old limiting habits. The Action phase is about practicing what we have changed into so that our brains and muscles and organs have a new constant to operate from.

One of the most challenging questions I can ask myself is "What am I practicing?" It is through this inquiry that I can locate myself. If I am practicing coming home at night after work and watching TV for four hours, then that is who I am: a worker and a vegetator. If I eat yummy vegetables, I am yummy. If I eat junk food, I am junk. We are what we eat, but more fundamentally, we are what we practice. If I am feeling dissatisfied with some aspect of my life, I have only to take stock of what I am practicing in order to locate myself and get onto the Moving Cycle, so that I can relocate myself on a different path. Bumper stickers tell us to practice random acts of kindness and senseless acts of beauty. Ministers exhort us to practice what we preach. In each case, practicing affirms and validates action.

What am I practicing? Sitting meditation is often called a practice. It involves the practice of finding space, the space between thoughts and the space around problems. Meditation locates us in space. Contemplative disciplines such as yoga, t'ai chi, calligraphy, archery, flower arranging, and tea cermony are all also practices designed to foster awakeness and present-centeredness.

What am I practicing? If I practice self-hatred, repeat it over and over throughout my day, I cannot help but become a hateful person. Self-hatred arises from the practice of self-hating more than it does from any horrible things we have done. How do I stop practicing something when I have been faithfully repeating it for so long that I don't know how to stop? The Moving Cycle provides the form, the container for stopping destructive or limiting practices. And the Action phase of the Moving Cycle helps us to begin practicing affirming, joy-producing behaviors that relocate us into more beautiful landscapes. The Action phase also aligns us toward further journeys on the Cycle. It positions us for deeper and more life-affirming travels on the spiral of life.

Our mind is analogous to a storehouse full of seeds. The seeds represent all the possible human feelings, opinions, and beliefs. We carry the seeds of hatred as well as love and caring. The issue of practice in our thinking, then, forms around the question "What seed am I watering?" As was said before, whatever we attend to will grow. For Hitler, the seeds of bitterness and hatred were watered by abusive parents, an impoverished childhood, and the social stresses of post–World War I Germany. And as an adult he kept watering these seeds instead of learning to water the others. We all have the capacity to do what Hitler did. But we have chosen, no matter what our childhood circumstances, to water different seeds.

When I work with clients or students, I pay close attention to what seeds they are watering. Good therapy is only partially about healing old wounds. It is also about changing one's orientation to life as it is right now. It is about choosing to water different seeds than we learned to water early on. Is my student not grasping this concept because it is too complex, or because she is watering her seeds of "I am stupid"? Is my client sad because a sorrowful thing has happened, or because she is watering seeds of sadness while she neglects her seeds of anger or joy? What kind of garden we live in depends on the kinds of seeds that sprout and grow.

The Action phase is also about turning in different attentional directions vis-à-vis our thoughts and beliefs. We have seen that we can weed out old limiting beliefs planted a long time ago by others. Now comes the task of planting and tending, and that is what action is for. If I want to be happier, I not only take care of and process my unhappiness, but I also cultivate my joy. I can begin by literally catching myself at being happy in small moments that I would have previously ignored. Instead of passing the feeling by, I bring the happy feeling onto the Moving Cycle. I wake up to it, own it as mine, and love it to pieces. I then reproduce it in the world. I might simply turn to the person next to me and tell them what I'm happy about. Or I might wiggle with it. What waters the seeds of your happiness? Whatever does, do it. Take action!

Exercises for the Action Phase

1. Take a leisurely walk. On this walk, practice oscillating your attention between your inner experience and what is going on around you. It is like the rhythm of breathing—attention in, attention out. Notice how your awareness of one affects and nourishes the other.

2. Repeat the same exercise, this time facing a partner. Oscillate your attention between your inner experience

and paying attention to the other person. Notice if you tend to get more focused on yourself or the other person. If your focus is unbalanced in either direction, use your breath as a guide: breathing in, sense yourself; breathing out, sense the other.

3. Make a list of what you are working to recover in your life right now. Be specific. After each item, write down something you'd like to do about it. If you are recovering your sense of humor, maybe you will decide to tell at least two jokes per day. Maybe you will take a class in stand-up comedy. If you are reclaiming your sexuality, you might want to read a book on sexual intimacy. Check to make sure that your do list is practical, do-able, and fun. Do it!

4. Tell others what you are recovering. When your friends, colleagues, and loved ones are alert to what your intentions are, they are more apt to witness you and affirm you when you manifest your recovery.

5. Spend time affirming what you care about in the world. Maybe it is the rainforest or hungry children or public radio or early childhood education. If you care about it, doing something to manifest that care will help you feel connected and hopeful. Perhaps you will want to donate time or money. Maybe you will write letters to elected officials. Whatever action you choose, monitor your sense of joy and satisfaction. If you are feeling angry or bitter about a world situation, go back to description and see if there is any sense of agenda or control attached to your action. If there is, work on it. Find an action that feels right for you, that expresses your recovery, that will contribute to the recovery of the world.

6. Do an integrity check. Have you broken any agreements or commitments, however small? Tell the truth

about it to yourself and to any affected people. Do what you can to make it right.

7. Take some time to write down the sentence "What do I practice?" and then make a list of any and all of the things you do in your day that tend to repeat. After each item on the list, write down who you are as you do it. This can be an opportunity to play with your inner characters. For instance, when I eat junk food I am usually in a hurry, tired and cranky, and not wanting to take care of myself ("Won't someone please materialize and cook my dinner for me?"). So, I feel at that point about five years old, not having had my nap, and being hurried off on some errand with my mother. I call this character Eugenia. I become Eugenia again and again every time I don't take time to eat well and end up at Taco Bell. My task then is to put Eugenia on the Moving Cycle. Locate your characters, and begin the Moving Cycle process. Celebrate locations that already feel life-affirming.

8. What practices might you like to take on that feel affirming of your highest purpose? Take some time to contemplate this. I recently put a t'ai chi class at the end of my two long work days. This has helped me to feel calm and centered and quietly alert where I used to come home to collapse, watch TV, and never get out of the exhausted feeling until I woke up the next day. You may wish to take on some kind of organized activity, or simply a regular easy walk, or a luxurious bath.

Conclusion
Singing the Body Electric

I celebrate myself, and sing myself,
And what I assume you shall assume,
For every atom belonging to me as good
*   belongs to you.*
    —WALT WHITMAN, *Song of Myself*

Recovering our bodies, whether from the depths of substance abuse or from quiet neglect, can be a reclamation of fundamental life. When we commit to staying in our direct current process, we vote for experiencing life in all its vivid glory. If we have abandoned our physical being consistently, our body will manifest a marker, a buoy-like movement or posture or gesture that can point us to the physical geography of our journey to recovery. It was following these movement markers that first alerted me to the importance of the body in any recovery process.

Recovery is a lifelong process, but not in the traditional sense. C. G. Jung once said that the unconscious is infinite. By this he meant that we would always be uncovering new material, new mysteries about ourselves. He saw us as lifelong astronauts, travelers on the road of inner exploration. It is in this sense that recovery takes the rest of our lives: once we recover what we have lost through trauma, abuse, or neglect, we don't need to stop there. We can continue recovering aspects of ourselves that we didn't know we had lost. Abraham Maslow stated that we have a basic human need to grow and transform, to seek ever higher states of consciousness. It is in this way that recovery can become a spiritual journey. When we commit to recovery, no matter what our starting point, we take a leap into space that can only result in our complete transformation.

Recovering our bodies is a lifelong process of commitment. There will always be new things to discover, because our bodies exist in the here and now, nowhere else. The here and now is always changing, always flowing. It is the only place where change can occur. By reclaiming our bodies, we reclaim the part of ourselves that is uniquely constructed to be our most fundamental mechanism of change, growth, and transformation. Until we construct a physical structure for our growth, our change processes have no home in which to live; emotional, cognitive, and spiritual change has no container to rest in, no home to dwell in. By starting with our bodies, we occupy a physical edifice that can be a home for emotional, cognitive, and spiritual growth. It is when we are not in this home that addiction can be a lifelong battle, a struggle to hold and keep our recovery when it has no body to live in.

We can distill four affirmations by which we can create the body container in which recovery and transformation can dwell.

The Four Affirmations

1. My feeling and sensing is an act of my aliveness, and the meaning of my aliveness is an exquisite mystery that reveals itself through my lifelong commitment to being fully present.

2. Everything I feel and sense is a part of me, and because it is created by me it is the source of my creativity.

3. Every part of me has its basis in love, because every feeling fully felt and truthfully expressed is inherently an act of love.

4. My aliveness and love find purpose and completion in my expression of them in the world.

These four affirmations are designed to stimulate and support the Moving Cycle in us. We can water the seeds of this moving, this daily homecoming process, by actively choosing it and by being alert for its natural emergence. Once we know that there are these four stages, once we witness and participate in them, we can consciously choose to go further forward and use the Moving Cycle as a means of deep exploration into our ultimately creative natures.

We begin with Awareness. Whether this starting point occurs out of some pain or suffering, or whether it shows up as an imperative for happiness, we can cradle the emergent experience and know that it will want next to be Owned, to be reassimilated. As we recover these parts of ourselves that we have pushed away or had not yet realized were there we reclaim wholeness. This wholeness must be greeted and loved and acknowledged; it needs our Acceptance into the fold of our aliveness, without conditions or limits. And to be complete, it must be made visible and manifest in the world through Action, through practice. In this way, by commiting to the cycle of life movement, we make our aliveness more important than any limits we previously assumed were required.

What am I making most important in my life? By commiting to cyclic movement back there in the shopping mall with the cookie, I began to make my direct experience of the world more important than my habit of repeating what I was used to. What we don't complete, we repeat. I had never completed some old feelings about food. I had never quite completed my feelings of fear of pleasure. I had not felt in my body the complete satisfaction of nourishment. And I had begun to make sugary substitutes more important than satisfying, complete experiences. I feared the death that comes when something is finished, truly over. When we haven't been fully alive, we fear death, we fear the open creative space that completion creates.

When I remember that state of quiet fear I used to live in, I get a tight, squeezing feeling on the sides of my upper throat. I say hello to it; I let it be there. I get curious, and I even intensify it in order to become more attuned to it. I can feel that if I were to let it go, I would cry. I allow it to hold the tears back, saying, "Yes, I know that you have been trying to dam up what you assumed would be a flood. Go ahead, it's OK. Now, are you sure it's a flood? Let's look; let's find out. Here we go, let's try breathing into the squeeze as much as we can." I breathe, my chest begins to shake a bit, and the tears come. As it turns out, it is not a flood, but a steady flow. I stay very awake, very committed to being absolutely truthful to their sensation and their expression. The tears come some more and with them my throat lets go. I smile to my throat, I smile to my tears. I see that the tears are a part of me that simply wanted to come home. No fuss. I feel now a sense of tingling in my upper chest, and I want to write about this profound little five-minute experience. Here, world, I am making myself visible, tangible, palpable. I move, I make ripples. My words come out of me, and behind them there is space. I wonder what will arise next?

I study with the Vietnamese Buddhist monk and teacher

Thich Nhat Hanh. One day he showed me a piece of paper. "Do you see this paper?" he said.

"Yes," I replied.

"Look deeply into it. Do you see also the logger who cut down the tree to make this piece of paper?"

"Yes. Without him the paper would not be here."

"Do you also see the wife of the logger who made his lunch the day he cut down the tree?"

"Yes."

"Do you see the truck that hauled the logs? The gasoline in the truck? The plants who died millennia ago to form the gasoline?"

"Yes."

"Look deeply. Is there anything that is not included in this piece of paper?"

"No."

We contain within ourselves the seeds of every quality, every feeling, every thing that exists. We house a universe of nascent possibilities. The seeds that we water will grow and shape us into a unique individual. How do we water these seeds? We start with Awareness, waking up to the vividness of everyday life. I knew I had recovered my awakeness when I spent time in the Arizona desert. For five days I felt drunk with the smell of the land, the colors of flowers, the thrum and buzz of hummingbirds, the feel of radiant heat on my skin. I realized, in the midst of my rapture, that the throb and pull of everyday life was sweeter than any external substance I had ever ingested, any high I had ever carefully arranged. I had come home to myself, and in so doing I had rekindled the world in what Diane Ackerman calls "all its gushing aliveness."

With Awareness, we can water the seeds of Owning. When we make the move from being self-absorbed to being self-responsible, we access all the power we need to transform ourselves into whoever we want to be. I am in a co-creative relationship with the world, a pas de deux of epic proportions. The power that arises from owning ourselves, all of ourselves, even the parts that haven't emerged yet, forms the fuel for the journey of recovery and transformation.

The seeds of love are perhaps the most pregnant with possibility. They are like the flowers of our inner landscape that make what we experience beautiful and full of breathtaking color. It is ultimately the act of loving ourselves unconditionally that brings us home both to ourselves and to others.

The seeds of action, when watered, bear fruit that feeds us all. We all live on the actions that we all produce. Life would cease if we didn't take action, in fact it is our movement, our actions, that even define that we are alive. The action of movement completes a cycle, whether it be a tricycle or the cycle of one's entire life.

Take a walk soon. Let yourself wander, taking in the sounds, sights, and smells around you. Now feel your body moving, its temperature, the pressure of the ground under your feet, the feeling of air going in and out of your lungs. Recovery is as simple and as stunning as this. Keep walking, and find where it takes you.

References

Ackerman, D. 1990. *A natural history of the senses.* New York: Vintage Books.

Beattie, M. 1987. *Codependent no more.* San Francisco: Harper/ Hazelden.

Black, C. 1981. *It will never happen to me.* New York: Ballantine Books.

Boadella, D. 1985. *Wilhelm Reich: The evolution of his work.* Boston: Arkana.

————. 1987. *Lifestreams: An introduction to biosynthesis.* New York: Routledge and Kegan Paul.

Bradshaw, J. 1987. *Bradshaw on the family: A revolutionary way of self-discovery.* Deerfield Beach, Fla.: Health Communications Publications.

————. 1988. *Healing the shame that binds you.* Deerfield Beach, Fla.: Health Communications Publications.

————. 1990. *Homecoming: Reclaiming and championing your inner child.* New York: Bantam Books.

Brown, M. 1990. *The healing touch: An introduction to organismic psychotherapy.* Mendocino, Calif.: LifeRhythm.

Cermak, T. L. 1986. *Diagnosing and treating codependence.* Minneapolis: Johnson Institute Books.

————. 1988. *A time to heal: The road to recovery for adult children of alcoholics.* Los Angeles: Jeremy P. Tarcher.

Christiansen, B. 1972. *Thus speaks the body.* New York: Arno Press.

Duncan, D. J. 1992. *The brothers K.* New York, Bantam Books.

Dychtwald, K. 1977. *Bodymind.* New York: Pantheon.

Freud, S. 1955. *The interpretation of dreams.* New York: Basic Books.

Gendlin, E. T. 1978. *Focusing.* New York: Everest House.

Grof, S. 1985. *Beyond the brain: Birth, death, and transcendence in psychotherapy.* Albany, N.Y.: SUNY Press.

Hanna, T. 1987. *The body of life.* New York: Alfred A. Knopf.

Hendricks, G., and K. Hendricks. 1990. *Conscious loving: The journey to co-commitment.* New York: Bantam Books.

————. 1991. *Radiance: Breathwork, movement, and body-centered psychotherapy.* Berkeley, Calif.: Wingbow.

————. 1993. *At the speed of life: A new approach to personal change through body-centered therapy.* New York: Bantam Books.

Jacobson, E. 1967. *Biology of emotions.* Springfield, Ill.: C. C. Thomas.

Janov, A. 1983. *Imprints: The lifelong effects of the birth experience.* New York: Coward-McCann.

Jellinek, E. M. 1981. *Alcohol addiction and the chronic alcoholic.* Manchester, N.H.: Ayer.

Johnson, D. 1983. *Body.* Boston: Beacon Press.

Kalat, J. W. 1988. *Biological psychology.* Belmont, Calif.: Wadsworth.

Keen, S. 1983. *The passionate life.* New York: Harper and Row.

Keleman, S. 1975. *Your body speaks its mind.* New York: Simon and Schuster.

————. 1985. *Emotional anatomy: The structure of experience.* Berkeley, Calif.: Center Press.

Kurtz, R. 1990. *Body-centered psychotherapy: The Hakomi method.* Mendocino, Calif.: LifeRhythm.

Kurtz, R., and H. Prestera. 1976. *The body reveals.* New York: Harper and Row.

Larsen, E. 1985. *Stage II recovery: Life beyond addiction.* San Francisco: HarperSanFrancisco.

————. 1987. *Stage II relationships: Love beyond addiction.* San Fransisco: HarperSanFrancisco.

Lerner, H. G. 1993. *The Dance of deception: pretending and truth-telling in women's lives.* New York: HarperCollins.

Levy, F. 1988. *Dance/movement therapy: A healing art.* Reston, Va.: The American Alliance for Health, Physical Education, Recreation, and Dance.

Lowen, A. 1965. *Love and orgasm.* New York: Signet Books.

————. 1970. *Pleasure: A creative approach to life.* New York: Penguin Books.

Miller, A. 1981. *The drama of the gifted child.* New York: Basic Books.

————. 1986. *Thou shalt not be aware.* New York: Meridian Books.

Mindell, A. 1982. *Dreambody: The body's role in revealing the self.* Boston: Sigo Press.

Murphy, M. 1992. *The future of the body.* Los Angeles: Jeremy P. Tarcher.

North, M. 1975. *Personality assessment through movement.* Boston: Plays, Inc.

Perls, F. 1969. *Gestalt therapy verbatim.* New York: Bantam Books.

Pesso, A. 1973. *Experience in action: A psychomotor psychology.* New York: SUNY Press.

————. 1969. *Movement in psychotherapy.* New York: New York University Press.

Pierrakos, J. C. 1987. *Core energetics.* Mendocino, Calif.: Life-Rhythm.

Reich, W. 1949. *Character analysis.* New York: Orgone Institute Press.

————. 1986. *The function of the orgasm.* New York: Farrar, Straus and Giroux.

Rosenberg, J., M. Rand, and D. Asay. 1985. *Body, self, and soul: Sustaining integration.* Atlanta: Humanics.

Saleebey, D. 1985. A social psychological perspective on addiction: Themes and disharmonies. *Journal of Drug Issues* (winter): 17–28.

Schneirla, T. C. 1959. An evolutionary and developmental theory of biphasic processes underlying approach and withdrawal. In *Nebraska symposium on motivation,* edited by M. R. Jones. Lincoln: University of Nebraska Press.

Smith, E. 1985. *The body in psychotherapy.* Jefferson, N.C.: Mc-Farland and Company.

Wegscheider, S. 1981. *Another chance: Hope and health for the alcoholic family.* Palo Alto, Calif.: Science and Behavior Books.

Wegscheider-Cruse, S. 1985. *Understanding me.* Deerfield Beach, Fla.: Health Communications.

Weis, A. 1989. *The aesthetics of excess.* New York: SUNY Press.

Whitfield, C. L. 1987. *Healing the child within: Discovery and recovery for adult children of dysfunctional families.* Deerfield Beach, Fla.: Health Communications.

Wikler, A. 1953. *Opiate addiction.* Springfield, Ill.: Charles C. Thomas.

———. 1973. Dynamics of drug dependence: Implications of a conditioning theory of research and treatment. *Archives of General Psychiatry* 28: 611–616.

Wilson-Schaef, A. 1985. *Codependence: Misunderstood-mistreated.* San Francisco: Harper and Row.

———. 1988. *When society becomes an addict.* San Francisco: Harper and Row.

Wilson-Schaef, A. and D. Fassel. 1990. *The addictive organization.* San Francisco: Harper and Row.

Wise, R. A., and M. A. Bozarth. 1987. A psychomotor stimulant theory of addiction. *Psychological Review* 94 (4): 469–492.

Woodman, M. 1982. *Addiction to perfection: The still unravished bride.* Toronto: Inner City Books.

Centers for
Body-Centered Psychotherapy

The Focusing Institute, Eugene Gendlin, Director. University of Chicago, 5848 University Ave., Chicago, IL 60637.

The Hakomi Institute, Ron Kurtz, Director. P.O. Box 1873, Boulder, CO 80306.

Hakomi Integrated Somatics, Pat Ogden, Director. P.O. Box 19438, Boulder, CO 80308.

The Hendricks Institute, Kathlyn Hendricks, Director. 120 North Tejon #203, Colorado Springs, CO 80903.

The Moving Center, Christine Caldwell, Director. P.O. Box 19892, Boulder, CO 80308

Rosenberg-Rand Institute of Integrated Body Psychotherapy (IBP), Marjorie Rand, Director. 1551 Ocean Ave., Suite 230, Santa Monica, CA 90401.